100

THINGS TO DO IN
PALM SPRINGS
BEFORE YOU
DIE

Date Palms
Courtesy of Palm Springs Bureau of Tourism

100

THINGS TO DO IN
PALM SPRINGS
BEFORE YOU
DIE

2nd Edition

LYDIA KREMER

REEDY PRESS

Library of Congress Control Number: 2018958380

ISBN: 9781681061917

Design by Jill Halpin

Cover Image: Tom Brewster Photography

Printed in the United States of America
18 19 20 21 22 5 4 3 2 1

Please note that websites, phone numbers, addresses, and company names are subject
to change or cancellation. We did our best to relay the most accurate information
available, but due to circumstances beyond our control, please do not hold us liable for
misinformation. When exploring new destinations, please do your homework before
you go.

DEDICATION

To my hero, Alex,
and to
the memory of my mother, Carmen,
who loved Palm Springs

• •

CONTENTS

• •

Music and Entertainment

• •

Culture and History

Shopping and Fashion

PREFACE

Welcome to the second edition of *100 Things to Do in Palm Springs Before You Die.*

The title is not intended literally but rather as a lighthearted aspirational endeavor. The title also echoes my long-held philosophy about Palm Springs: when you visit, "you'll think you've died and gone to heaven!" And you won't be alone; countless wayfarers and adventurers have discovered that there are way more than one hundred reasons why Palm Springs is a world-renowned, glamorous, and fun destination.

This second edition includes even more reasons to love Palm Springs. There are some new eateries, new shopping venues, and other ways to entertain yourself in our magnificent destination. Palm Springs's new downtown core has a new Kimpton hotel, the Rowan; a bevy of shopping opportunities; and several new eateries. Down Valley, economic boom times are also evident with new shops, hotels, and restaurants. This is a great time to visit and/or revisit Palm Springs!

Located approximately one hundred miles east of Los Angeles, Palm Springs is an oasis in the Southern California desert, known for its breathtaking mountain vistas, its diverse and picturesque landscape, and its casual but stylish vibe. The poolside cocktail hour is a highlight of the day and an opportunity to make a Palm Springs-style fashion statement—in fact "desert casual" is part of the vernacular for party invitations in Palm Springs!

• •

Upon arriving, you'll soon realize that "Palm Springs" is used broadly to refer to the entire Coachella Valley, an area approximately thirty-five miles in length that comprises nine cities, each with its own cultural identity. The nine cities, from west to east, are: Palm Springs, Desert Hot Springs (slightly north), Cathedral City, Rancho Mirage, Palm Desert, Indian Wells, La Quinta, Indio, and Coachella.

We are a seasonal community: we go full tilt during "season," which is typically from about October through May. During summer we downshift to a slower pace, although there are still plenty of activities to enjoy—for visitors this means great rewards, such as visitor-friendly bargains and hotel rates.

The beauty of Greater Palm Springs is a visually seductive image that will have you longing to return often. The soaring Santa Rosa and San Jacinto Mountains National Monument, with 10,000-foot peaks, creates a stunning backdrop. It might inspire you to relocate here, as so many others have done.

In any case, I hope you'll find this guide to be a useful checklist of one hundred ways to celebrate and indulge yourself. Welcome to heaven!

—Lydia Kremer

• •

ACKNOWLEDGMENTS

There is compelling proof that it's the colorful, fascinating, generous, and creative people who cross our paths that make life such a rewarding journey. To all whom I've encountered, befriended, toasted, or had a convivial conversation with during my decades in Palm Springs, I send my gratitude and admiration.

Special thanks to the Greater Palm Springs cities—Palm Springs, Palm Desert, La Quinta, Indian Wells, and Indio— that provided photos and assisted with content. My thanks also to the Palm Springs Bureau of Tourism, and particularly Tom Brewster, for the images in this book.

Lastly, to my tribe—thank you to my family, friends, and colleagues—you fill my heart.

FOOD AND DRINK

CELEBRATE
PALM DESERT FOOD AND WINE

Discriminating palates won't have to look too far to get a foodie fix in Palm Springs. The desert communities boast a sophisticated culinary scene, where you'll discover a variety of annual events that elevate dining and imbibing to an art.

The most notable annual event is Palm Desert Food and Wine, which takes place each March. This glamorous food and wine celebration is produced by *Palm Springs Life* magazine and features more than two hundred food, wine, and spirits purveyors. The event offers cooking demonstrations, chef book signings, numerous receptions with celebrity chefs, and a prestigious James Beard Luncheon featuring celebrated chefs, who prepare an unforgettable four-course lunch.

760-325-2333
palmdesertfoodandwine.com

INSIDER'S TIP

Palm Springs Life magazine has been the voice of the desert communities for more than sixty years. Pick up the latest copy during your visit to get up to speed on the current happenings in music, film, fashion, events, shopping, dining, design, real estate, and much more.

SAMPLE TASTY TREATS

Greater Palm Springs hosts numerous food-centric events throughout the year. The Greek Festival (two days in February) is sponsored by the St. George Greek Orthodox Church of Palm Desert. This popular annual event marked its twentieth anniversary in 2016 and will continue the tradition of celebrating all things Greek—authentic Greek food, live bouzouki music, and Greek dancing. The Rhythm, Wine, and Brews Experience (March) is an outdoor beer and wine fest featuring samples of craft beers and wine, with more than forty breweries and thirty wineries from around the state. Food trucks and live music add to the fun. The Taste of Summer Rancho Mirage gives visitors a chance to enjoy special pricing at participating restaurants.

Greek Festival
St. George Greek Orthodox Church
74-109 Larrea, Palm Desert
760-568-9901
pdgreekfest.org

Rhythm, Wine, and Brews Experience
Empire Polo Club
81800 Ave. 51, Indio
760-342-2762
rwbexp.com

Taste of Summer Rancho Mirage
tasteofsummerranchomirage.com

WHAT'S COOKIN'
AT LE VALLAURIS?

A hands-on culinary experience with a cooking demonstration is a fun opportunity to enjoy wonderful cuisine in a whole new way. Le Vallauris, the premier French restaurant in Palm Springs, has been a fine-dining destination in the desert for more than forty years. From November to May, it offers monthly cooking demonstrations by executive chef Jean Paul Lair and pastry chef Laurent Dellac. Enjoy a fabulous three-course meal following the demonstration and take home a booklet of the recipes.

385 W. Tahquitz Canyon Way, Palm Springs
760-325-5059
levallauris.com

TASTE TRADITION
AT TAMALE FESTIVAL

The Indio International Tamale Festival is a two-day event celebrating the rich cultural heritage of the humble tamale, which varies wildly within cultures, and even within families, but is always a delectable treat. You can sample dozens of tamales, from sweet to savory and from vegetarian to gluten free. The festival, held in the heart of Old Town Indio, takes place annually the first weekend in December. Founded in 1992, the festival has received numerous accolades, most notably the Food Network's Top 10 list of "All-American Food Festivals." It has also been included in *Guinness World Records* for the world's largest tamale (one foot wide and forty feet long) and the largest tamale festival based on attendance (120,000).

760-262-4633
tamalefestival.net

SEE CAMEL RACES
AT DATE FESTIVAL

At the ten-day Riverside County Fair and National Date Festival (February), you'll find a variety of tasty treats made with dates. The festival, an annual tradition since 1946, features a carnival atmosphere and family fun, with nightly musical performances by notable artists. It also has camel rides, as well as seven thousand exhibits and booths offering crafts, food, and beverages. One of the highlights of the event is the crowning of Queen Scheherazade, a nod to the Middle Eastern origin of the date. You can sample a surprising variety of dishes made with the biblical fruit—candy, baked goods, jam, and more. Be sure to try a scrumptious date shake, a local specialty.

Riverside County Fairgrounds, 82-503 Highway 111, Indio
800-811-3247
datefest.org

FUN FACT

Dates were introduced to the Coachella Valley at the turn of the last century as part of an effort by the US Department of Agriculture to find crops from around the world that could be grown in the United States. Seedlings were brought to the Coachella Valley from the Middle East, and, due to the region's high temperatures and low humidity, dates have flourished. Date palms are iconic fixtures in the eastern portion of the Coachella Valley and a major boon to the economy of the region. Today, dates are an important (and delicious) agricultural industry in the area.

FIND YOUR NEW BEST
CRAFT BEER

The craft beer movement in Greater Palm Springs is well established and has several local breweries you'll want to visit for a taste and a tour. Babe's Bar-B-Que and Brewhouse has been brewing award-winning tasty hops since the early 2000s and has been a trendsetter in the desert. The legacy of the late founder, Don Callender, who also founded the Marie Callender's restaurant chain, is savored in every sip. Coachella Valley Brewing Co. uses a state-of-the-art, seventeen-barrel brewhouse—a HEBS, or high-efficiency, brewing system, one of only five such systems in the world. This high-tech process enables the brewery to produce a variety of stellar award-winning brews from locally sourced ingredients. La Quinta Brewing Co. has three taprooms, with a new one in downtown Palm Springs, and produces several brews that have also won top honors statewide.

Babe's Bar-B-Que and Brewhouse
71800 Hwy. 111, Rancho Mirage
760-346-8738
babesbbqandbrewhouse.com

Coachella Valley Brewing Co.
30640 Gunther St., Thousand Palms
760-343-5973
cvbco.com

La Quinta Brewing Co.
Brewery Taproom, 77917 Wildcat Dr., Palm Desert
760-200-2597

301 N. Palm Canyon Dr., Palm Springs
760-200-2597

78-065 Main St. #100, La Quinta
760-972-4251
laquintabrewing.com

EAT, DRINK, AND BE MERRY
AT RESTAURANT WEEK

Another culinary highlight is Palm Springs Desert Resorts Restaurant Week. You'll be singing the praises of the fabulous dining scene here, and if you time your visit right, you'll be able to eat your way through the desert cities for a song. Each year in June, Restaurant Week takes place throughout the desert cities, when local favorite restaurants offer a prix fixe lunch and dinner for bargain prices that you won't want to pass up. You'll be able to choose from two hundred eateries—bistros, cafés, diners, and fine-dining establishments. Restaurant Week also partners with many of the local hotels, which offer great rates and packages.

760-322-8008 or 760-770-9000
palmspringsrestaurantweek.com

SIP COCKTAILS
ON ROOFTOPS

Watching the sun slip behind the mountains and seeing the light change to mauve and purple is a thrilling sight and a highlight of the day in Palm Springs. And what could be better than celebrating this daily ritual from a rooftop vantage point while enjoying a cocktail? High Bar, located on the seventh floor at the Kimpton Rowan Hotel, is the highest rooftop pool/bar in Palm Springs and offers a sweeping 360-degree panorama along with its signature craft cocktails to toast the start of a festive evening. La Serena Villas, a restored 1930s hotel, also has a roof deck called Sugar High, upstairs from the hotel's restaurant called Azúcar (meaning sugar in Spanish). Get it? Enhance your "sugar high" with a variety of specialty cocktails, brews, and tasty bites.

High Bar at the Kimpton Rowan Hotel
100 W. Tahquitz Canyon Way, Palm Springs
760-904-5015
rowanpalmsprings.com

Sugar High Roof Deck at La Serena Villas
339 S. Belardo Rd., Palm Springs
844-932-8044
laserenavillas.com

TOAST
THE COCKTAIL HOUR

When the clock strikes five, it's time to participate in one of the desert's most coveted sports—happy hour! Whether your style is a friendly neighborhood pub, a stylish modern bar, or a classic throwback watering hole, you'll find the perfect place for cocktails to fit your mood. There are several notable possibilities you should put on your list, and if your sunset happy hour runs into the dinner hour, so much the better. Some of these notable suggestions offer postcard views, adventuresome libations, fun retro design, or poolside DJ parties, but all offer a convivial atmosphere.

Libation Room
73750 El Paseo #101, Palm Desert
877-869-8891
libationroom.com

Truss and Twine
800 N. Palm Canyon Dr., Palm Springs
760-699-7294
trussandtwine.com

Ace Hotel
701 E. Palm Canyon Dr., Palm Springs
760-325-9900
acehotel.com/palmsprings

INSIDER'S TIP

If you are planning to imbibe a few cocktails, take advantage of the Buzz, a complimentary shuttle service in the City of Palm Springs. The colorful Buzz trolley makes several stops in a loop from one end of town to the other. The free Buzz program has trolleys that run every fifteen to twenty minutes Thursday, Friday, and Saturday from noon to 10 p.m.

Search the route at sunline.org.

DINE
AL FRESCO

Thanks to 360 days of sunshine, dining al fresco while happily ensconced on an outdoor patio is de rigueur in Palm Springs. Accordingly, numerous restaurants in the desert communities have lush outdoor patios, most of which offer heaters in winter and cooling misters in summer to keep guests comfortable year-round. Besides serving meals outdoors, some restaurants in downtown Palm Springs offer great opportunities for our favorite sport: people-watching. In each of the Greater Palm Springs cities, there are countless possibilities for grabbing a casual meal or having a fine-dining experience while enjoying the desert sunshine or evening air. The following are just a few eateries that have outdoor patios, great menus, and a friendly, welcoming atmosphere.

Eight4Nine Restaurant and Lounge
849 N. Palm Canyon Dr.
Palm Springs
760-325-8490
eight4nine.com

Pomme Frite
256 S. Palm Canyon Dr.
Palm Springs
760-778-3727
pommefrite.com

Tommy Bahama and Marlin Bar
111 N. Palm Canyon Dr., #150
Palm Springs
760-778-0012
tommybahama.com/restaurants/
palm-springs-marlin-bar

Spencer's
701 W. Baristo Rd.
Palm Springs
760-327-3446
spencersrestaurant.com

INSIDER'S TIP

Here's a tip for navigating your way through the Coachella Valley. California State Highway 111 runs through eight of the nine cities that make up Greater Palm Springs. While searching for a particular address on Highway 111, be sure you identify in which city the business is located. Also note that in Palm Springs the main thoroughfare is called Palm Canyon Drive, with sections of the street referred to as North Palm Canyon Drive, East Palm Canyon Drive, or South Palm Canyon Drive. If you are trying to locate a business on Palm Canyon Drive, make note whether the address is North, South, or East Palm Canyon Drive, and you'll find your destination more easily.

GRAB A CUP OF JOE

The nation's trend for coffee snobbery certainly hasn't passed Greater Palm Springs by. Whether you're looking for a java jolt as a quick pick-me-up in the afternoon or wanting a leisurely morning cuppa with your pals to catch up, there's a perfect spot for you just minutes away from your location in the desert. One of the most popular coffee hangouts is Koffi, with four locations in Palm Springs and Rancho Mirage. In the heart of downtown Palm Springs, you'll find the Starbucks Reserve, where you can sit at a bar and choose your brew from many global coffee regions and any number of brewing options. The east part of the Coachella Valley also serves up satisfying java. At Vintage Coffee House you can enjoy light fare with your cup of joe.

Koffi
four locations
kofficoffee.com

Starbucks Reserve
110 N. Palm Canyon Dr., Palm Springs
760-318-2287
starbucksreserve.com

Vintage Coffee House
49990 Jefferson St., Indio
760-564-2407

START YOUR ENGINES
WITH BREAKFAST

Just like Mom told you, don't skip breakfast: it's a celebration to begin your day and jump-start your engine. Whether you want a "grab 'n go" or a comforting full breakfast Mom would be proud of, there are several standout breakfast restaurants around the desert cities. Wilma and Frieda is a great spot to fortify yourself before a day of shopping at the Gardens on El Paseo. Elmer's has been a local favorite since 1960. A more recent local fave is Cheeky's, which offers a changing, creative menu—a bacon flight is a house specialty. La Quinta Baking Company features a bakery and casual French fare. Don and Sweet Sue's Café is a local go-to for comfort food in Cathedral City.

Wilma and Frieda
73575 El Paseo Dr., Palm Desert
760-773-2807
wilmafrieda.com

Elmer's
1030 E. Palm Canyon Dr., Palm Springs
760-327-8419
eatatelmers.com

Cheeky's
622 N. Palm Canyon Dr., Palm Springs
760-327-7595
cheekysps.com

La Quinta Baking Company
78395 Hwy. 111, La Quinta
760-777-1699
laquintabaking.com

Don and Sweet Sue's Café
68-955 Ramon Rd. #1, Cathedral City
760-770-2760
donandsweetsues.com

REV UP
YOUR CULINARY ADVENTURE

As an ever-growing tourism destination, Greater Palm Springs is constantly adding exciting eateries to its dynamic culinary scene. Nearly forty new restaurants have opened just in Palm Desert in the last two years! There's a dining establishment suited to your tastes, whatever they may be—whether casual, fine dining, grab 'n go, or a leisurely meal to enjoy the desert ambiance, we've got you covered. So check out these new kids on the block that have added to the buzz around the desert communities.

Each of these new eateries is worth a try. The Pink Cabana is visual delight with a Mediterranean-Moroccan influenced menu. For adventurous dining and killer views, 4 Saints won't disappoint. Beyond Belisage is Chef Daniel Villanueva's newest exciting culinary adventure.

The Pink Cabana, Sands Hotel and Spa
44-985 Province Way, Indian Wells
760-321-3771
sandshotelandspa.com

4 Saints, Klimpton Rowan Hotel
100 W. Tahquitz Canyon Way, Palm Springs
760-392-2020
4saintspalmsprings.com

Amanda's Tea Room
73625 Hwy. 111, Suite C, Palm Desert
760-341-4101
amandastearoom.com

Grand Central
160 La Plaza, Palm Springs
760-699-7185
grandcentralpalmsprings.com

Heirloom Craft Kitchen
49990 Jefferson St., Indio
760-773-2233
heirloomcraftkitchen.com

Beyond Balisage
68-327 E. Palm Canyon Dr., Cathedral City
760-699-8536
danielstable.com

Chúla Artisan Eatery
47150 Washington St., La Quinta
760-227-6616
chulaeatery.com

INDULGE YOURSELF
WITH FINE DINING

Fine dining in the desert has been elevated to the status of a VIP special event. You'll find an array of exceptional fine dining establishments here, with sophisticated cuisine to satisfy any foodie. Here are just a few standouts, both large and small, and all equally wonderful. Johannes has a menu of excellent European and Austrian food inspired by chef/owner Johannes Bacher's roots. Lavender Bistro, a family-owned restaurant, has its roots in exceptional French cuisine. The Steakhouse doubles your pleasure with two locations, and it's not just for dinner anymore—the Steakhouse also serves a fabulous Sunday brunch. Wally's Desert Turtle has been a fine-dining institution in the desert since 1978. Dining at Le Vallauris, located off the beaten path, is a culinary celebration that won't disappoint.

Johannes
196 S. Indian Canyon Dr., Palm Springs
760-778-0017
johannesrestaurants.com

Lavender Bistro (dinner only)
78-073 Calle Barcelona, La Quinta
760-564-5353
lavenderbistro.com

The Steakhouse
Agua Caliente Casino Resort Spa
32-250 Bob Hope Dr., Rancho Mirage
hotwatercasino.com

Spa Resort Casino
401 E. Amado Rd., Palm Springs
sparesortcasino.com
888-999-1995

Wally's Desert Turtle
71775 Hwy. 111, Rancho Mirage
760-568-9321
wallysdesertturtle.com

Le Vallauris
385 W. Tahquitz Canyon Way, Palm Springs
760-325-5059
levallauris.com

TAKE THE BURGER CHALLENGE

As with many things in life, everyone has their own criteria for what makes the perfect burger. It's all in the eye of the B-holder. But it can be fun trying to find your own favorite, so take the burger challenge and decide for yourself. Whether you go for the sloppy ones piled high with exotic toppings or just a classic burger, there's a place for you. Here are just a few local burger joints.

From elegant (Purple Palm) to a wide range of options (fifty choices at Tony's Burgers). you won't go wrong at any of these local burger spots.

Purple Palm Restaurant at
Colony Palms Hotel
572 N. Indian Canyon Dr., Palm Springs
760-969-1818
purplepalmrestaurant.com

Grill-A-Burger
73091 Country Club Dr., Palm Desert
760-346-8170
grill-a-burger.com

Smokin' Burgers and Lounge
1775 E. Palm Canyon Dr.,
Suite 220, Palm Springs
760-883-5999
smokinburgers.com

Tony's Burgers
35903 Date Palm Dr., Cathedral City
760-832-7794
tonysburgers.com

Burgers and Beer
72773 Dinah Shore Dr., Rancho Mirage
760-202-4522
burgersandbeer.com

DROP IN
FOR TYLER'S BEST BUNS

Because hamburgers are an original Southern California tradition (McDonald's and In-N-Out started here), it's not surprising that Tyler's in Palm Springs has been touted as one of the top five burger joints in the state. The Zagat-rated eatery, located in the historic La Plaza in downtown Palm Springs, is in a league of its own for burgers and hot dogs. Tyler's offers straightforward and delicious burgers and sliders with a choice of sides, including its signature potato salad and its coleslaw, which has been described as legendary. Pair your burger with Tyler's freshly made lemonade or indulge yourself with an old-fashioned milkshake. The place is only open for lunch and accepts strictly cash. Warren Buffett and Bill Gates have been known to drop in for burgers and a meeting of minds. The line at Tyler's speaks for itself but is well worth the wait. Be sure to check before you go; Tyler's is closed for a few weeks in the summer.

149 S. Indian Canyon Dr., Palm Springs
760-325-2990
tylersburgers.com

GET YOUR SWEET TOOTH ON

What would a day be without a sweet indulgence? Sure, you'll find See's Candies in a couple of Coachella Valley locations, but give our locally produced handcrafted candies a try. Palm Springs Fudge and Chocolates was originally called Heiminger's when it opened in 1994 and featured fudge from Mackinac Island, Michigan. It is still family operated and prides itself on the highest-quality old-fashioned fudge, truffles, toffee, and chocolates. Brandini Toffee began as a fundraising effort for two high school pals, who turned their award-winning almond toffee recipe into a nationally known product now found at retailers around the country, including twenty-five West Coast Nordstroms. Drop by the Rancho Mirage facility for a tour or swing by the Palm Springs Toffee Shop for a free sample—you'll be hooked.

Brandini Toffee Shop and Factory
42250 Bob Hope Dr.
Rancho Mirage
760-200-1598
brandinitoffee.com

Brandini Toffee Shop
132 S. Palm Canyon Dr.
Palm Springs
760-200-1598
brandinitoffee.com

Palm Springs Fudge and Chocolates
211 S. Palm Canyon Dr., Palm Springs
760-416-0075
palmspringsfudgeandchocolates.com

SAY CIAO BELLA

Maybe it's because Ol' Blue Eyes demanded excellent, authentic Italian food while he lived in Palm Springs that the desert communities have such exceptional Italian cuisine. Many current restaurants would make Mr. Sinatra proud. Owned by two Castelli brothers, Castelli's Ristorante has been consistently voted a locals' favorite. Among the house specialties that garner raves are chef Brian Altman's fettuccini alfredo. The owners of Il Giardino brought their excellent authentic Northern Italian cuisine directly to Palm Springs from Milan after relocating in 2015. Johnny Costa's menu features some of Frank Sinatra's favorite dishes, which Mr. Costa was invited to personally prepare at Sinatra's home. Family-run Spaghetteria Pasta and Pizza features terrific food and is a friendly neighborhood eatery where "Mama" may bid you hello from the kitchen. La Spiga Ristorante's menu features everything made from scratch, with high-quality organic ingredients.

INSIDER'S TIP

Because Greater Palm Springs has been an international tourist destination for decades, we have no shortage of international cuisine options to choose from. Your palate can take a trip around the world with the range of restaurants specializing in a variety of ethnic and international cuisines.

Castelli's Ristorante
73-098 Hwy. 111, Palm Desert
760-773-3365
castellis.cc

Il Giardino
333 S. Indian Canyon Dr., Palm Springs
760-322-0888
ilgiardinopalmsprings.com

Johnny Costa's
440 S. Palm Canyon Dr., Palm Springs
760-325-4556
johnnycostaspalmsprings.com

Spaghetteria Pasta and Pizza
611 S. Palm Canyon Dr., Palm Springs
760-322-7647

La Spiga Ristorante
72-557 Hwy. 111, Palm Desert
760-340-9318
laspigapalmdesert.com

TASTE SAVORY MEXICAN

If you're hankering for tasty Mexican fare, each of the nine cities in Greater Palm Springs can claim some of the best Mexican food in Southern California. I've narrowed down the options with a disclaimer: these are not the only great Mexican eateries. The El Mexicali Café, the oldest woman-owned Mexican eatery in the desert, serves authentic, tasty Mexican food at three locations. The next best thing to a taco truck is El Jefe, which serves delectable street tacos at the Saguaro Hotel. Las Casuelas Terraza has been an institution since 1958. At the Spotlight 29 Casino, La Diabla Maria serves authentic street-style tacos and tequila flights. Rincón Norteño is another fifty-year-plus tradition. Off the beaten path in Palm Springs, but worth a visit, is La Perlita. In Desert Hot Springs, the owner of South of the Border is a renowned retired matador.

Las Casuelas Terraza
222 S. Palm Canyon Dr., Palm Springs
760-325-2794
lascasuelas.com

El Mexicali Café
82720 Indio Blvd., Indio
760-347-1280
elmexicalicafe.com

Rincón Norteño
83-011 Indio Blvd., Indio
760-347-4754
rinconnorteno.com

La Diabla Maria
Spotlight 29 Casino
46-200 Harrison Pl., Coachella
760-775-5566
spotlight29.com

La Perlita
901 Crossley Rd., Palm Springs
760-778-8014
laperlitamexicanfood.letseat.at

South of the Border
11719 Palm Dr., Desert Hot Springs
760-251-4000

EXPAND YOUR HORIZONS
WITH ASIAN CUISINE

Greater Palm Springs also has its share of restaurants specializing in wonderful Asian food. Peppers Thai serves reliably delectable Thai specialties at reasonable prices. Thai Smile serves savory Thai dishes with a refined and relaxing ambiance. City Wok is the desert outpost of an LA chain that serves great made-to-order Chinese. In Desert Hot Springs, Thai Palms Restaurant has been serving healthy, genuine Thai cuisine for fifteen years. For Vietnamese cuisine, try Rooster and the Pig, whose menu features classic Vietnamese specialties with an American twist. This place has a lively atmosphere with a full bar and house cocktails. Or check out Viet-fusion Pho 533, which serves fresh, healthy, and savory Vietnamese pho, banh mi sandwiches, spring rolls, and more. The original owner named it Pho 533 for Land Transport Tanker 533, the vessel that carried her and her family from war-torn Vietnam to America in 1975.

Peppers Thai Cuisine
396 N. Palm Canyon Dr., Palm Springs
760-322-1259
peppersthai.com

Thai Smile Palm Springs
100 S. Indian Canyon Dr., Palm Springs
760-320-5503
thaismilepalmsprings.com

City Wok
74970 Country Club Dr., Palm Desert
760-341-1511
citywok.com

Thai Palms Restaurant
12070 Palm Dr., Desert Hot Springs
760-288-3934
thaipalmdhs.com

The Rooster and the Pig
356 S. Indian Canyon Dr., Palm Springs
760-832-6691
roosterandthepig.com

Pho 533
1775 E. Palm Canyon Dr., Suite 625, Palm Springs
760-778-6595
pho533palmsprings.com

JOIN LOS COMPADRES
FOR DEEP PIT BBQ

The annual Deep Pit Barbeque at Los Compadres, a not-to-be-missed local tradition since 1949, reflects a bit of Palm Springs's equestrian history. Los Compadres is one of the oldest riding clubs in Palm Springs; its membership spans several generations of local families. The private club throws its doors open to the public once a year for this "Old West" event. Held the first weekend in November, the barbeque features beef that is slow-cooked for twenty-four hours in a six-foot-deep cement barbeque pit. The event, held outdoors at the Los Compadres clubhouse, is a fun and festive evening with music and frivolity. The Western BBQ feast is served with ranch beans, coleslaw, and homemade cookies. Beer and wine are available for purchase, too.

1849 S. El Cielo Rd., Palm Springs
760-322-2218
loscompadresclub.com

SIP WINE
AT DESERT WINES AND SPIRITS

Wine enthusiasts should head to Desert Wines and Spirits for wine tastings held each Saturday from 4 to 5:30 p.m.; there's a $10 charge for the tasting, but $5 of that can be applied to any purchase. Hosted by owners Costa and Zola Nichols, these convivial wine tastings are fun gatherings of residents and visitors alike who share the love of wine. Even if you aren't too knowledgeable about wine, you are guaranteed to leave a lot smarter. Each week, Costa, one of the foremost wine experts in the area, curates a special wine tasting that showcases a different wine, varietal, or country. The Tasting Room is open for individual or group tastings every day. Go Deli and Gourmet Market is also on-site and offers great sandwiches and the perfect items for pairing.

611 S. Palm Canyon Dr., Suite 22, Palm Springs
760-327-7701
desertwinesandspirits.com

BE CASUAL

If you're looking for a casual environment but don't want to compromise on the quality of food, you're in luck. Greater Palm Springs has a multitude of great unfussy eateries to fit your taste, mood, and budget. Many of these spots are local favorites. Since 1976, John's Restaurant has been the perfect place to drop in for a hearty breakfast, a quick lunch, or a casual dinner. Place your order at the counter and grab a seat, and your order appears quickly. Enjoy expansive views in the courtyard at MidMod Café, which has brought fresh, organic, healthy fare to the Uptown Design District. Jake's is a local favorite with a friendly atmosphere.

John's Restaurant
900 N. Palm Canyon Dr., Palm Springs
760-327-8522
johnsrestaurantpalmsprings.com

MidMod Café
515 N. Palm Canyon Dr., Palm Springs
760-699-7714
app.midmodcafe.com

Jake's
664 N. Palm Canyon Dr., Palm Springs
760-327-4400
jakespalmsprings.com

DELIGHT
AT LOCAL DELIS

Sometimes you need the good old-fashioned comfort food found in authentic delis. Take your big appetite to Sherman's Deli, which has two locations—its original location in Palm Springs and its sister property in Palm Desert. A New York–style deli, it has a sandwich board featuring forty enormous sandwiches, such as its famous corned beef, as well as kosher items for breakfast, lunch, and dinner. This family business has been a local tradition since 1963. Sherman's also features tempting baked goods and pastries, all made on the premises. And Manhattan in the Desert, as the name implies, will take your taste buds back to your childhood. This New York–style delicatessen serves breakfast, lunch, and dinner.

Sherman's Deli and Bakery
]401 E. Tahquitz Canyon Way, Palm Springs
760-325-1199
73-161 Country Club Dr., Palm Desert
760-568-1350
shermansdeli.com

Manhattan in the Desert
2665 E. Palm Canyon Dr., Palm Springs
760-322-3354
manhattaninthedesert.com

The Swing N Hops
Courtesy of the City of Palm Desert

MUSIC AND ENTERTAINMENT

DISCOVER RAT PACK FAME
AT PURPLE ROOM

Known as one of the Rat Pack's Palm Springs hangouts, the Purple Room is a stylish retro supper club that opened in 1960. It features live entertainment and a full dinner menu. Enjoy nightly happy hour and complimentary entertainment on Tuesdays, Wednesdays, Thursdays, and late night on Fridays, or make it date night for the Purple Room's Mainstage ticketed shows on most Friday, Saturday, and Sunday evenings. Reservations are required for table seating for the Mainstage dinner shows, but you can snag a barstool and belly up to the bar to enjoy the show.

1900 E. Palm Canyon Dr., Palm Springs
760-322-4422
purpleroompalmsprings.com

FUN FACT

Palm Springs has long been the glamorous playground for countless stars who escaped the glare of Hollywood, a tradition that continues today. One of the early celebrities was Frank Sinatra, who first arrived in Palm Springs in the 1940s. In 1947, he built a home that became a magnet for many of his pals—Dean Martin, Sammy Davis Jr., Peter Lawford, and Joey Bishop—who collectively became known as the Rat Pack. Local tales about the fun-loving pals' antics are legendary.

DANCE TIL YOU DROP

Drop in to the Casablanca Lounge at Melvyn's Restaurant any night of the week for free live music and dancing, and you just might rub elbows with a celebrity. Located at the historic Ingleside Inn, Melvyn's has been a magnet for celebrities throughout its forty-plus-year history. Melvyn's is one of the only remaining vestiges of Old Palm Springs. Things have remained the same, with just a little refreshing here and there; in fact, you may think you're in a '70s disco time warp.

If you ever had a notion to dance in the streets, here's your chance. Dust off your dancing shoes for a rocking street party in Palm Desert. The annual Swing 'N Hops Street Party, held each February, takes over the El Paseo shopping street with a beer garden, gourmet food trucks and booths, a vintage car show, and, of course, music to swing to. If your moves are rusty, no worries; there will be some dance instruction, too. The event is part of the First Weekend series of Palm Desert celebrations and features a live swing band and a dance floor. Of course, you'll want to wear duds from the swing era to enhance your fun.

Casablanca Lounge at
Melvyn's Restaurant
200 W. Ramon Rd., Palm Springs
760-325-2323
inglesideinn.com/melvyns

Swing 'N Hops
El Paseo, Palm Desert
palm-desert.org/events/swing-n-hops

MUSIC'S IN THE AIR
AT COACHELLA

Palm Springs is renowned for inhabiting the intersection of fun, glamour, and sunshine. Those attributes offer the ideal backdrop for its dynamic music scene and major music festivals. Among the world's granddaddies of music festivals is the Coachella Valley Music and Arts Festival, held on two consecutive weekends each April at the Empire Polo Club in Indio. Since its inaugural event in 1999, Coachella has grown exponentially and now draws more than 200,000 attendees from around the globe. While it's still dedicated to its alternative musical roots, Coachella features a variety of musical genres. Coachella has also morphed into an important launchpad and showcase for artists. The event's mix of major international headlining acts and emerging new talent has made this the most successful music festival in the world. Accordingly, tickets sell out fast.

81-800 Ave. 51, Indio
888-512-7469
coachella.com

ENJOY MORE
MUSIC FESTIVALS

The Coachella Valley Music and Arts Festival might not be your cup of tea, but not to worry; no matter what your musical tastes, you'll be sure to find a music festival in the desert that will be just the thing. Goldenvoice, the force behind Coachella, also produces the Stagecoach Country Music Festival, a three-day fest that takes place a few weeks after Coachella in the same location at the Empire Polo Club in Indio. The Palm Springs Women's Jazz Festival (September) brings together legendary female jazz musicians and up-and-coming jazz talents for multiple days at the Annenberg Theater; it culminates with a Sunday brunch. The Joshua Tree Music Festival (May and October), billed as a "family-friendly global music experience," throws in art, yoga, and organic foods to round out the four-day high-desert music fest.

Stagecoach Country Music Festival
81-800 Ave. 51, Indio
stagecoachfestival.com

Palm Springs Women's Jazz Festival
101 Museum Dr., Palm Springs
760-416-3545
pswomensjazzfestival.com

Joshua Tree Music Festival
joshuatreemusicfestival.com

CELEBRATE
THE WHITE PARTY

Palm Springs is one of the country's largest gay enclaves, and the annual White Party during spring break is the largest gay dance party in the world. Founded by impresario Jeffrey Sanker, the event is an over-the-top fun bacchanalia that draws thirty thousand men for three days of events in various venues around Palm Springs, featuring renowned celebrity DJs, live performances by international artists, pool parties, and more. Although there are White Parties in other locations, Palm Springs is ground zero for this global celebration.

Historically, the White Party has presented major entertainers such as Christina Aguilera, Jennifer Lopez, Lady Gaga, and Belinda Carlisle. Besides three days of dance parties, there is a carnival featuring a midway with a Ferris wheel and vendor booths. The event culminates with the desert's largest choreographed fireworks display set to music.

jeffreysanker.com/white-party-palm-springs

CATCH
PERFORMING ARTS
AT MCCALLUM THEATRE

The McCallum Theatre, named for a local pioneering family, was among the very earliest performing and cultural arts entities in Greater Palm Springs. Since its auspicious opening night in 1988—a star-studded affair attended by the likes of Bob Hope, former president Gerald Ford, Lucille Ball, and Sarah Brightman—the McCallum Theatre has presented world-class music, dance, theater, comedy, and opera performances each season since. The elegant theater, with a capacity of 1,127, is a cultural gem in the desert and is a valued community and educational partner. The McCallum Institute is a philanthropic arm of the theater whose mission is promoting the arts to local children and students. Among the notable headliners appearing at the McCallum have been Michael Feinstein, Plácido Domingo, Shirley MacLaine, Kenny G, and many other legendary entertainers.

73000 Fred Waring Dr., Palm Desert
760-340-2787
mccallumtheatre.com

CELEBRATE
FREE CONCERT SERIES

Grab a picnic lunch and head to the Great Lawn at Sunnylands Center and Gardens for its annual Music in the Gardens free concert series every Sunday afternoon in March. The concert series features vocalists and musicians who perform a variety of musical genres, including jazz, blues, classical, pop, and more. The City of Rancho Mirage presents Music in the Park, its free concert series that draws many renowned entertainers and is held outdoors in the evening desert air. The free Desert Hot Springs Classical Concert Series is presented by pianist and recording artist Danny Holt, who curates a season of wonderful entertainment.

Sunnylands Center and Gardens
37977 Bob Hope Dr.
Rancho Mirage
760-202-2222
sunnylands.org

Desert Hot Springs
Classical Concerts
17400 Bubbling Wells Rd.
Desert Hot Springs
dannyholt.net/dhs-classical-concerts

Music in the Park
Rancho Mirage Amphitheater
71560 San Jacinto Dr.
Rancho Mirage
760-324-4511
ranchomirageca.gov/music-in-the-park-concert-series

ENJOY AN OASIS
FOR LIVE PERFORMANCE

In addition to the McCallum Theatre, you will find many more performing arts venues, both large and small, that offer a broad spectrum of music, theater, and more. Among the other venues are the Annenberg Theater, located in the lower level of the Palm Springs Art Museum, which presents a variety of productions including some of Broadway's best, and the Coachella Valley Repertory Theatre (CVREP) a nonprofit theater that will soon be housed in a new home (check the website). Dezart Performs is another nonprofit organization that produces high-quality theater; the Palm Canyon Theatre is an intimate theater setting in a historic building that presents Broadway musicals and classical productions; and the Indio Performing Arts Center features music, comedy, and stage productions.

Annenberg Theater
101 Museum Dr., Palm Springs
760-325-4490
psmuseum.org/annenberg-theater

Coachella Valley Repertory Theatre
760-296-2966
cvrep.org

Dezart Performs
760-322-0179
dezartperforms.org

Palm Canyon Theatre
538 N. Palm Canyon Dr.
Palm Springs
760-323-5123
palmcanyontheatre.org

Indio Performing Arts Center
45175 Fargo St., Indio
760-391-4174
indioperformingartscenter.com

GRAB A CHAIR
AT OPERA IN THE PARK

Love Mozart, Verdi, and Puccini? As the saying goes, the best things in life are free, and such is the case with the annual Opera in the Park, which has been a beloved springtime tradition in Palm Springs since 1998. Produced by the Palm Springs Opera Guild of the Desert, it is a much-anticipated annual event for families and people of all ages who may not be opera fans but who love seeing outdoor performances by a talented cast of professional opera singers accompanied by a live orchestra. Attendees are invited to bring chairs, blankets, and picnics to enjoy a pleasant afternoon under the trees, listening to the voices of angels singing favorite opera arias. And, of course, it's free!

401 S. Pavilion Way, Palm Springs
760-325-6107
palmspringsoperaguild.org

DISCOVER ENTERTAINMENT
AT TRIBAL VENUES

One of the many unique aspects that makes Greater Palm Springs a culturally vibrant experience is that some areas either sit on or are adjacent to tribal reservations. Each tribal reservation here boasts a world-class casino/resort that presents a variety of high-caliber entertainment. The Agua Caliente Band of Cahuilla Indians has two such venues—Spa Resort Casino in Palm Springs and Agua Caliente Spa Resort Casino in Rancho Mirage. The Cabazon Band of Mission Indians has Fantasy Springs Resort Casino in Indio, and Spotlight 29 Casino in Coachella is a business venture of the Twenty-Nine Palms Band of Mission Indians. Each of these venues presents major headliners in comedy, pop, rock 'n roll, big band, hip-hop, tribute performers, illusionists, and more. Check their websites for schedules and tickets.

Spa Resort Casino
401 E. Amado Rd., Palm Springs
888-999-1995
sparesortcasino.com

Spotlight 29 Casino
46-200 Harrison Place, Coachella
760-775-5566
spotlight29.com

Agua Caliente Casino Resort Spa
32-250 Bob Hope Dr.
Rancho Mirage
888-999-1995
hotwatercasino.com

Fantasy Springs Resort Casino
84-245 Indio Springs Pkwy., Indio
800-827-2946
fantasyspringsresort.com

ENJOY EVENTS
AT RANCHO MIRAGE LIBRARY

Many of us grew up thinking of libraries as quiet places that existed strictly to explore the world of books and information. No longer. To experience the dramatic evolution of how libraries have become vital community gathering places, head over to the Rancho Mirage Public Library, which provides local residents and visitors alike with wonderful cultural programs. The range of engaging public events is broad and includes film screenings, lectures, concerts, exhibits, family nights, children's story times, book discussions, and more. A music concert in a library? Yup. The library presents an International Classical Concert Series, as well as many other musical performances throughout the year. Some of the concerts have an admission fee, but many programs are free.

71-100 Hwy. 111, Rancho Mirage
760-341-7323
ranchomiragelibrary.org

SPORTS AND RECREATION

WATCH TENNIS PROS
AT BNP PARIBAS

If it's March in Greater Palm Springs, you should head to the BNP Paribas Open at the Indian Wells Tennis Garden to catch all the top-tier tennis players in the world. The tournament, held each year in early March, is the first of nine ATP World Tour Masters series events and is held in one of the world's best tennis stadiums. The Indian Wells Tennis Garden, owned by billionaire Larry Ellison, co-founder of the Oracle Corporation, is the world's second- largest tennis venue. During the past couple of years, Ellison has invested a hefty sum to upgrade and add additional tennis stadiums and amenities to enhance the visitor experience tenfold. Situated on nearly sixty acres, the Indian Wells Tennis Garden features two state-of-the-art stadiums with 24,000 seats, plus dining, shopping, and entertainment, all in a stunning setting.

78-200 Miles Ave., Indian Wells
760-200-8400
bnpparibasopen.com

TAKE A THRILL RIDE
AT AERIAL TRAMWAY

The Palm Springs Aerial Tramway is a unique year-round thrill ride. The Aerial Tramway, opened in 1963, has the world's largest rotating tramcars. The cars take visitors on a 2.5-mile ride up the side of the mountain, from the desert floor to a pine forest, in ten minutes, during which riders experience a temperature difference of thirty to forty degrees. Along the ride, a recorded narration gives you some of the history and background of this marvel. Your journey begins at the Valley Station, at an elevation of 2,643 feet, and ends at the Mountain Station, at an elevation of 8,516 feet. You're transported to the Mount San Jacinto State Park, with fifty miles of hiking trails, ideal for picnicking and enjoying outdoor adventure. The Mountain Station offers two restaurants, a gift shop, and a terrace with awe-inspiring views.

1 Tramway Rd., Palm Springs
888-515-8726
pstramway.com

TAKE A ROAD TRIP
TO THE SALTON SEA

One of the best ways to experience the natural beauty and diverse environment of the Greater Palm Springs region is from behind the wheel, and there are several notable scenic drives to choose from. Take Highway 10 to Highway 86 approximately thirty miles east out to the Salton Sea, the second-largest lake in California. The Salton Sea Recreation Area offers fishing, boating, camping, and excellent bird watching. Be sure to stop at the Visitors Center on the north side of the lake. Or, take the Palms to Pines Scenic Byway (Highway 74), an extraordinary sixty-seven-mile drive. Start out in Palm Desert on Highway 74; stop at Vista Point for sweeping views and continue on the road as it winds through forests and snow-capped mountains to the charming mountain village of Idyllwild, which is worth a visit.

Salton Sea State Recreation Area
100-225 State Park Rd., Mecca
760-393-3052
parks.ca.gov/?page_id=639

Palms to Pines Scenic Byway
Highway 74
909-382-2600
fs.usda.gov/recarea/sbnf/recarea/?recid=26521

INSIDER'S TIP

If you want a scenic drive, definitely put the mountain arts community of Idyllwild on your list of things to do. From the desert cities of the Coachella Valley, Idyllwild is only an hour's drive but a world away. You can take one of two routes. Situated at an elevation of nearly six thousand feet, Idyllwild offers a tranquil respite in a forest setting, with great hiking, dining, arts, music, shopping, and wine tasting.

idyllwild.com

WALK IN ANCIENT FOOTSTEPS
AT INDIAN CANYONS

When you visit Palm Springs, you may be surprised to realize you are on the site of a sovereign Indian nation. The Agua Caliente Band of Cahuilla Indians has inhabited the region for five centuries, and its 31,000-acre reservation extends to swaths of Palm Springs, Cathedral City, and portions of Rancho Mirage. The most significant sites on the reservation are Indian Canyons, four distinct canyons—Palm Canyon, Murray Canyon, Andreas Canyon, and Tahquitz Canyon. They offer thoroughly sublime scenery where you can hike among streams, pools, waterfalls, and the world's largest fan palm oasis. Indian Canyons are listed on the National Register of Historic Places and are considered sacred land by this tribe, which requires respectful use of the canyons.

38500 S. Palm Canyon Dr., Palm Springs
760-323-6018
indian-canyons.com

HIKE
THE THOUSAND PALMS OASIS

Before the railroad, the site of the Thousand Palms Oasis at the Coachella Valley Preserve was a major stagecoach stop between the Colorado River gold mines and Los Angeles. Today the Thousand Palms Oasis, situated in the 18,000-acre Coachella Valley Preserve System, is a great recreational outpost with picnicking, guided tours, and more than twenty-five miles of hiking trails. Besides seeing a variety of rare habitats, you'll discover the preserve's fascinating geological and anthropological history. Inhabited by various Indian cultures for centuries, the preserve has cool ponds and springs that are fed from the famed San Andreas earthquake fault, which you can visit on a guided tour. Be sure to stop at the historic Palm House Visitors Center, a rustic 1930s–40s building that contains educational information about the natural and historic features of the area.

29200 Thousand Palms Canyon Rd., Thousand Palms
760-343-2733
coachellavalleypreserve.org

FUN FACT
You'll see a large variety of palm trees throughout the Coachella Valley, but the palms that are present in the region's natural oases are *Washingtonia filifera*, commonly referred to as the California fan palm. Among 2,500 species of the world's palms, the fan palm is the only palm native to California.

CATCH A FISH
AT WHITEWATER PRESERVE

The Whitewater Preserve is a pristine, scenic riparian habitat on 2,800 acres located just northwest of Palm Springs. Under the aegis of the Wildlands Conservancy, the Whitewater Preserve is adjacent to the San Gorgonio Wilderness and is home to many native flora and fauna species. The Whitewater River will soon be designated a National Wild and Scenic River, pending legislation. Whitewater Preserve and its environs are open daily for hiking, picnicking, permit camping, and catch-and-release fishing with permit. There is a visitor and ranger station with informational and educational materials to enhance your visit, such as trail maps and lists of flowers, birds, and reptile and amphibian species you may be able to spot. For seasoned hikers, there is a trailhead connecting to the Pacific Crest Trail.

9160 Whitewater Canyon Rd., Whitewater
760-325-7222
wildlandsconservancy.org/preserve_whitewater.html

TAKE THE PLUNGE

Poolside recreation in Greater Palm Springs is practically a religion. There are several swim centers for visitors, who can drop in at their leisure to enjoy the facilities. The Palm Desert Aquatic Center is an eight-acre facility at the Palm Desert Civic Park with three pools for lap swimming and swim and fitness classes, as well as water polo. The Palm Springs Swim Center features an Olympic-sized outdoor pool for year-round lap swimming, recreational swimming, and aquatic programs for all ages. The Swim Center is located adjacent to the city-operated Leisure Center. The John Furbee Aquatic Center in Desert Hot Springs offers open swimming and swim classes.

Palm Desert Aquatic Center
73751 Magnesia Falls Dr., Palm Desert
760-565-7467
cityofpalmdesert.org/departments/parks-recreation/aquatic-center

Palm Springs Swim Center
405 S. Pavilion Way, Palm Springs
760-323-8278
palmspringsca.gov/government/departments/parks-recreation/swim-center

John Furbee Aquatic Center
11750 Cholla Dr., Desert Hot Springs
760-329-6411 x 219
cityofdhs.org/aquatics

VENTURE
INTO THE SAN ANDREAS FAULT

Take one of the many San Andreas Fault tours to see the renowned earthquake fault that inspires such enormous fascination. This geological wonder, which dates back twenty-eight million years, traverses the length of the Coachella Valley and is an intriguing attraction. Tours to the legendary fault, offered by several tour operators, are guided excursions in either closed or open-air Jeeps and Hummers. Tour guides are naturalists who are knowledgeable about the geology, history, and flora and fauna of the area. You'll see ancient canyons that have been twisted over time by Mother Nature. Be sure to check the websites for a list of things to take along on your Jeep excursion.

Desert Adventures Red Jeep Tours
74-794 Lennon Place, Palm Desert
760-324-5337
red-jeep.com

Big Wheel Tours
42160 State St., Palm Desert
760-779-1837

1590 S. Palm Canyon Dr., Palm Springs
760-548-0500
bwbtours.com

DISCOVER
THE LIVING DESERT'S WILD SIDE

For a fun day communing with the natural world, enjoy an adventure at Palm Desert's The Living Desert Gardens and Zoo, which emphasizes education, conservation, and preservation. Established in 1970, The Living Desert has grown to 1,200 acres, of which 1,000 acres are a preserve featuring an undeveloped area of Sonoran desert in its natural state. Walk along the nature trails to see more than 300 species from Africa, Australia, and North America. There are live animal shows, tram rides, sprawling gardens, and a model train exhibit. The botanical gardens represent plants from the Southern California desert, as well as from other regions of the world. The Living Desert also offers cafés, gift shops, and a garden center where you can purchase rare plants.

47900 Portola Ave., Palm Desert
760-346-5694
livingdesert.org

CATCH A FALLING STAR
IN JOSHUA TREE

The absence of big-city lights in the desert region makes it ideal for stargazing. In nearby Joshua Tree National Park, you will find some of the darkest skies in Southern California, which allow awe-inspiring views of the Milky Way, constellations, planets, and, during certain times of the year, spectacular meteor showers. The National Park Service at Joshua Tree offers nighttime stargazing throughout the year. In celebration of the one hundredth anniversary of the National Park Service in 2016, Joshua Tree began a Night Sky Festival; call or check the website for more info. The Gargan Optics Observatory is a private, state-of-the-art, climate-controlled observatory that offers group stargazing shows by reservation. Experience the thrill of peering at the cosmos through a massive, research-grade, GPS-guided robotic telescope. Open Thursday through Sunday.

Joshua Tree National Park
74485 National Park Dr., Twentynine Palms
760-367-5500
nps.gov/jotr/planyourvisit/stargazing.htm

Gargan Optics Observatory
72727 Jack Kramer Lane, Indio
760-238-4584
garganoptics.space

OBSERVE THE COSMOS
AT THE RANCHO MIRAGE OBSERVATORY

Adding to its already diverse programming, which includes lectures, films, and concerts, the Rancho Mirage Library opened a state-of-the-art observatory in March 2018. That's right, the Rancho Mirage Library may be the only library in the country to have its very own observatory and resident astronomer!

The Rancho Mirage Observatory's 700mm telescope is open for free public tours, stargazing events, films, and other observatory programs. The PlaneWave Instruments CDK700 telescope can observe objects more than fifty million light years away, essentially farther than three trillion times the distance between the Earth and the Sun.

To take a free tour of the observatory or to attend any of the stargazing parties, check the schedule and book online.

71-100 Hwy. 111
Rancho Mirage
760-341-7323
ranchomiragelibrary.org/observatory.html

SEE HORSEPLAY
AT LOCAL POLO CLUBS

Polo in the desert? We've got that, too. In fact, there has been world-class polo in the Coachella Valley for more than fifty years at two renowned polo clubs—the Eldorado Polo Club and the Empire Polo Club, both in Indio. During the season, from January to April, you can watch professional polo games every Sunday that are open to the public. Parking is $10, but admission for the polo games is free. You can purchase food and beverages or make it a fun tailgate picnic. At Eldorado you can enjoy a meal or drinks while watching the polo games from the Clubhouse or the Cantina. Polo is fast-paced and thrilling to watch; the games are held on an enormous, verdant green field the size of nine football fields.

Eldorado Polo Club	**Empire Polo Club**
50950 Madison St., Indio	81-800 Ave. 51, Indio
760-342-2223	760-342-9111
eldoradopoloclub.com	empirepolo.com

INSIDER'S TIP
The Empire Polo Club is also the site of the annual Coachella Valley Music and Arts Festival, the largest music festival in the world, which is held over two weekends in April. The free Sunday polo games are suspended at the beginning of April to accommodate the more than 200,000 attendees of Coachella.

VISIT NEW
NATIONAL MONUMENTS

After a ten-year effort by US Senator Dianne Feinstein, Greater Palm Springs now boasts three new national monuments. In 2016, President Obama designated the Sand to Snow National Monument, Castle Mountains National Monument, and Mojave Trails National Monument, and in so doing he protected an additional 1.8 million acres of diverse natural habitat that now create an unbroken corridor for many animal species, including bighorn sheep, tortoises, and fringe-toed lizards. Because the monuments cover a sweeping area, you can access them in various locations. The three monuments contain volcanic spires, dunes, ribbons of wetlands wedged between steep canyon walls, grasslands, Joshua tree forests, ancient petroglyphs, and the historic Route 66. Check the website for specific access points and recreational areas.

nps.gov/archeology/sites/antiquities/monumentslist.htm

TAKE A SOUND BATH
AT INTEGRATRON

A short twenty-minute drive from Joshua Tree, the Integratron will reward you with the unique experience of a "sound bath" in an "acoustically perfect" dome sited on a powerful geomagnetic vortex. The Integratron was designed and built in the 1950s by George Van Tassel, a UFO theorist, to enhance rejuvenation, anti-gravity, and time travel, supposedly from instructions he received from visitors from the planet Venus. How's that for quirkiness? The Integratron was financed by donations, including funds from another eccentric, Howard Hughes. Under the present ownership, the Integratron is open for "sound baths" in the sound chamber, during which a sequence of quartz crystal singing bowls, which are keyed to the body's energy centers, are played. Visits are by reservation only, but you can bring a picnic to enjoy the grounds.

2477 Belfield Blvd., Landers
760-364-3126
integratron.com

INSIDER'S TIP

If vortices are your thing, the city of Desert Hot Springs is known to have numerous locations that are attributed to the convergence of five energies: earthquake faults, geothermal underground water, mountain peak alignments, wind, and sun energies. The city is also renowned for its hot springs spas. So if you don't encounter a vortex, you can rejuvenate your spirit in the city's many natural hot springs.

TOUR THE WINDMILLS

You've likely seen all the windmills on the western edge of Palm Springs, but you can view them up close and personal on a windmill tour. The ninety-minute to two-hour tour takes you inside the gates of the private property, where scores of operating windmills are located. Palm Springs Windmill Tours has headquarters on the site, where you can view a gallery of historic photos. The tour also includes an outdoor exhibit of various windmill designs of the past thirty-five years, and you'll learn why some were successful and others not so much. You'll get an interesting overview of the sustainable wind energy industry and other forms of alternative energy, including solar and natural gas. The tours are conducted by a knowledgeable guide in an enclosed, air-conditioned passenger van.

62950 Twentieth Ave., Palm Springs
442-333-7188
windmilltours.com

FUN FACT

The San Gorgonio Pass, located to the west of Palm Springs, is considered one of the windiest places in Southern California. This creates an ideal location for the windmill industry, which explains why so many windmills dot the surrounding landscape.

TEE OFF
AT WESTIN MISSION HILLS

Considered a golfer's paradise, the Coachella Valley has you covered whether you're an avid or occasional golfer. With more than 120 golf courses and resorts, you won't find yourself far from a green. To keep up your golf swing, check out these top public courses. Westin Mission Hills offers two stellar courses: the Pete Dye Resort Course and the Gary Player Signature Course, both top-caliber championship courses. Indian Wells Golf Resort completed an $80 million renovation to make the Celebrity Course and the Players Course the ultimate golf experiences. Desert Willow Golf Resort's Mountain View Course is a municipal golf course owned by the City of Palm Desert, with all the amenities of a top private facility. The Indian Canyons Golf Resort's South Course has spellbinding views of Mount San Jacinto.

**Pete Dye Resort Course and
Gary Player Signature Course,
Westin Mission Hills Resort**
Rancho Mirage
760-328-3198
playmissionhills.com

**Celebrity Course and Players Course,
Indian Wells Golf Resort**
Indian Wells
760-346-4653
indianwellsresort.com

Mountain View Course, Desert Willow Golf Resort
Palm Desert
760-346-0015
desertwillow.com

South Course, Indian Canyons Golf Resort
Palm Springs
760-833-8724
indiancanyonsgolf.com

GOLF
UNDER THE STARS

With more than 120 golf courses, Greater Palm Springs has provided golf aficionados the best of all worlds—world-class championship courses, stunning landscapes, and enviable year-round weather. But the golf experience has just gotten even better—nighttime golf has come to Greater Palm Springs!

The Indio Golf Course, the only night-lighted golf course, offers "Play the Lights," a thrilling new golf experience under the stars. Complete with sweeping fairways and a full-length driving range, the course is suited to any skill level. "Play the Lights" is perfect for busy folks who are challenged to fit in time for golf.

The Indian Wells Golf Resort caters to night owls with its Shots in the Night, an interactive laser putting game, from sunset until 10 p.m.

Indio Golf Course
83040 Ave. 42, Indio
760-391-4049
indiogolf.com

Indian Wells Golf Resort
44-500 Indian Wells Lane, Indian Wells
760-346-4653
indianwellsgolfresort.com

TAKE THE WATERS
IN DESERT HOT SPRINGS

If soaking your stress away is your idea of a good time, take a sojourn to Desert Hot Springs, world-renowned for its healing mineral hot springs, hence the name. Located just north of Palm Springs, Desert Hot Springs is situated on one of the world's only hot and cold mineral spring aquifers, percolating from a depth of three hundred feet below the surface. These geothermal mineral waters are known to have many health benefits, which attract visitors from around the globe.

Desert Hot Springs, whose motto is "Hot Is Our Middle Name," has more than a dozen resort spas—from expansive to intimate, from glam to family-friendly, from extravagant to easy-on-the-budget. These resorts offer you the opportunity to luxuriate in these natural hot mineral waters, in addition to providing an array of pampering spa services.

visitdeserthotsprings.com

WATCH THE GOLF PROS
AT FRANK SINATRA INVITATIONAL

If you prefer golf as a spectator sport, the Greater Palm Springs area has a long history of playing host to some of the country's most prestigious professional golf tournaments, not to mention the bold-faced names that have enjoyed the links in the Coachella Valley, including former presidents Dwight D. Eisenhower, Bill Clinton, and Barack Obama; Bob Hope; Frank Sinatra; and many others. While most of the original tournament names have changed over the years with new title sponsors, there are many tournaments throughout the season where you can observe the world's best pro golfers mix it up with celebrities. Here are just a few annual tourneys.

The **CareerBuilder Challenge** (in January),
formerly the Bob Hope Classic, continues
Hope's legacy of raising funds for local charities.
careerbuilderchallenge.com

The **Frank Sinatra Celebrity Invitational**
(in February) was founded in 1986 by Sinatra to
benefit the Barbara Sinatra Center for Abused Children.
franksinatracelebritygolf.org

LPGA ANA Inspiration (in March/April),
one of five major LPGA events, was formerly the
Dinah Shore/Kraft Nabisco Championship.
anainspiration.com

DO YOGA
AT SUNNYLANDS

There's no reason to forgo your yoga practice while visiting Coachella Valley. Head to Sunnylands Center and Gardens for a free hour-long class held on the expansive lawn each Friday morning during the season. These free yoga classes are conducted by Kristin Olson, a respected yoga instructor for nearly forty years, and the classes are suitable for all levels. You can't help being inspired by the outdoor setting, surrounded by spectacular gardens and magnificent views of the soaring Mount San Jacinto. But if you miss these Friday yoga classes, you can still get in some exercise by walking the 1.25 miles of trails that meander through Sunnylands' sublime gardens.

37977 Bob Hope Dr., Rancho Mirage
760-202-2222
sunnylands.org

PEDAL FOR CHARITY
AT TOUR DE PALM SPRINGS

The Tour de Palm Springs, an annual signature cycling event in Palm Springs since 1999, draws 8,000 riders and 25,000 spectators from around the country. Held in January/February, the Tour de Palm Springs raises funds for several charities. Sponsored by Coachella Valley Serving People in Need (CVSPIN), this cycling event has raised more than $3 million as of 2016. The two-day event offers riders a choice of ride lengths—five, ten, twenty-five, fifty, or one hundred miles. Walkers may also participate in 1.5- or 3-mile routes. The routes take riders throughout the streets of Palm Springs and through surrounding scenic areas. The event also features a vendor expo in downtown Palm Springs.

760-674-4700
To register: tourdepalmsprings.com

TAKE A BALLOON RIDE
AT HOT AIR BALLOON FESTIVAL

The Cathedral City Hot Air Balloon Festival began in 2015 but quickly became a popular event for family-friendly fun. Held in February to coincide with Valentine's Day, the Balloon Festival hosts three days of activities that take place in various locations and venues, including Cathedral City's Civic Park. The festival features balloon tether rides, special event dinners, musical entertainment, gourmet food trucks, and a Kids' Zone. A highlight is the nighttime balloon glow event, with nearly thirty hot air balloons that are lit up to music during a forty-five-minute show. General admission to the festival is free; however, tickets and/or passes are required to participate in certain activities and access VIP areas. The event is organized by Fantasy Balloon Flights, which operates balloon rides from October to May if you miss the event in February.

Cathedral City Hot Air Balloon Festival—Cathedral City Town Center
68-700 Avenida Lalo Guerrero, Cathedral City
(check website for dates and other locations)
hotairballoonfest.com

Fantasy Balloon Flights
760-568-0997
fantasyballoonflight.com

WATCH THE PEOPLE PARADE
IN DOWNTOWN PALM SPRINGS

One of the most popular activities in Greater Palm Springs is the sport of people-watching—and it's absolutely free. In fact, people-watching is a very popular sport, particularly along Palm Canyon Drive in downtown Palm Springs. To snag a front-row seat for the "people parade," head to any number of the pubs, bistros, and eateries with relaxing outdoor patios that dot Palm Canyon Drive. Here are just a few.

Lulu California Bistro
200 S. Palm Canyon Dr.
Palm Springs
760-327-5858
lulupalmsprings.com

TRIO
707 N. Palm Canyon Dr.
Palm Springs
760-864-8746
triopalmsprings.com

Peabody's Café
134 S. Palm Canyon Dr.
Palm Springs
760-322-1877
peabodyscafeandbar.com

Zin American Bistro
198 S. Palm Canyon Dr.
Palm Springs
760-322-6300
pszin.com

TAKE AN OUTBACK
ADVENTURE HUMMER TOUR

Venture off the beaten path with Adventure Hummer Tours to see the mesmerizing desert landscape up close and personal. You'll be in for an off-roading adventure in an open-air H1 Hummer or an enclosed, luxurious H2 Hummer with military-grade suspension for a smooth ride. The company offers tours to many destinations, including Joshua Tree National Park, that include lunch or dinner for a value-added experience. The adventure tours to Joshua Tree take you a mile high in the back country, where you can see ancient rock formations, a variety of animal life, and the world-famous Joshua trees, which can live to be a thousand years old. Adventure Hummer Tours can accommodate private groups or corporate groups of any size.

760-285-0876
adventurehummer.com

82

TAKE TO THE SKIES
WITH PALM SPRINGS BIPLANES

Experience the thrill of flying in a restored vintage 1940 Stearman biplane for an unparalleled bird's-eye view of the Coachella Valley. Palm Springs Biplanes offers exciting open-cockpit rides for one or two persons. The tours—the fifteen-minute Barnstormer, the thirty-minute Coachella Coaster, or the one-hour Southern Cross—fly over different portions of the Coachella Valley's picturesque desert and mountain landscape. Palm Springs Biplanes can even arrange to document your flight with a digitally recorded video as a special keepsake.

145 N. Gene Autry Trail, Palm Springs
760-216-3700
psbiplanes.com

CELEBRATE A PARADE

Greater Palm Springs is a community that loves parades. For all seasons this community finds a reason to have a parade.

But Palm Springs itself has the most parades; here are just a few. Veterans Day in Palm Springs (the largest in Southern California) has been a tradition for more than two decades and includes a parade on Palm Canyon Drive, a patriotic concert, and a fireworks show. The first Saturday in December is the Festival of Lights Parade, which draws 100,000 spectators. The LGBTQ community is celebrated in both Palm Springs and Desert Hot Springs. Desert Hot Springs has its own Holiday Parade, too.

For more than fifty years, the City of Palm Desert has presented its annual Golf Cart Parade on El Paseo. It's a wacky and fun event that starts off with a pancake breakfast and ends with an awards presentation.

City of Palm Springs
Veterans Day Parade
ci.palm-springs.ca.us

City of Palm Springs
Festival of Lights
psfestivaloflights.com

City of Desert Hot Springs
Holiday Parade
cityofdhs.org

City of Palm Springs
Pride Festival and Parade
pspride.org

City of Desert Hot Springs
Pride Festival
dhspride2018.org

City of Palm Desert
Golf Cart Parade
golfcartparade.com

BE A ROCK STAR
AT DESERT ROCKS CLIMBING GYM

Want to test your endurance and stamina? Prove your mettle at Desert Rocks Indoor Climbing Gym for an exhilarating adventure. It's both a gym and a place for recreational fun that is suitable for all ages and fitness levels. The facility has seven thousand square feet of space, with two twenty-eight-foot walls for harness climbing in the main room. There is also a seventeen-foot bouldering wall for unharnessed climbing, but don't worry, there is a foam pad underneath for your safety. A second room, available for private events, features another wall for beginning climbers. It's open seven days a week year-round, so even during the summer months you can enjoy an indoor rock-climbing experience in an air-conditioned environment. Yoga and fitness classes are also available.

19160 McLane St., Palm Springs
760-671-1101
climbdesertrocks.com

RIDE THE WAVES
AT WET 'N WILD

Palm Springs might be about a hundred miles from the Pacific Ocean, but you can still experience a little of the California surf lifestyle at Wet 'n Wild Palm Springs, a large water park with a variety of rides for all ages. Hop onto Wet 'n Wild's FlowRider, which simulates perfect surf waves. Try the Pipeline with its three slides—an open-body slide, an open-tube slide, and an enclosed-body slide. Or check out the thrill of the gravity-defying speed slides on the Tidal Wave Towers, which are seven stories high. Kahuna's Beach House is a four-story family fun house with interactive water jets and more. Private cabanas, food concessions, and wading pools for tots make this great family fun from March to October.

1500 S. Gene Autry Trail, Palm Springs
760-327-0499
wetnwildpalmsprings.com

TRY YOUR LUCK
AT A CASINO

Try your luck in one of Coachella Valley's many gaming casinos, where you'll find Las Vegas–style gaming. There are several glamorous casinos on sovereign tribal reservations with hotels, dining, and entertainment, plus slot machines and a variety of table games. On the east end of the valley, Spotlight 29 Casino features 1,600 slot machines, plus five-dollar tables and slot and blackjack tournaments. Just down the road you'll find Fantasy Springs Resort Casino, with 2,000 slot machines, video poker, and forty table games. Mid-valley is the Agua Caliente Casino Resort Spa, where you can enjoy slots, table games, a high-limit room, and a poker room. In downtown Palm Springs, at the Spa Resort Casino, you'll be able to enjoy gaming 24/7 with slots, table games, and more.

Spotlight 29 Casino
46-200 Harrison Place, Coachella
760-775-5566
spotlight29.com

Fantasy Springs Resort Casino
84-245 Indio Springs Dr., Indio
760-342-5000
fantasyspringsresort.com

Agua Caliente Casino
32-250 Bob Hope Dr.
Rancho Mirage
888-999-1995
hotwatercasino.com

Spa Resort Casino
401 E. Amado Rd., Palm Springs
888-999-1995
sparesortcasino.com

RELIVE THE WILD WEST
AT PIONEERTOWN

Just a thirty-two-mile scenic drive from Palm Springs is a slice of the Old West at Pioneertown, an authentic Hollywood creation built in 1946. Pioneertown is a perfectly preserved full-scale town built as a motion picture set. The town comprises several rustic structures, including a corral, a marshal's office, a church, and other facades, as well as a working post office and shops. The Pioneertown Motel, originally built to house actors and crew, can be rented for overnight stays, so you can check in and stay a spell. Pioneertown served as a set and backdrop for numerous television shows and Western films, including *The Cisco Kid*, a 1950s TV show. Pioneertown has a few shops and hosts shoot-out reenactments. Don't miss Pappy and Harriet's Pioneertown Palace for great grub and live music.

5240 Curtis Rd., Pioneertown
760-365-7001
pioneertown-motel.com

GET BACK IN THE SADDLE
AT SMOKE TREE STABLES

If you're hankering for a bit of the cowboy way, Smoke Tree Stables can put you in the saddle again. Palm Springs had a robust equestrian culture in its early days, and Smoke Tree Stables has been organizing trail rides since 1927. The stables are located adjacent to 150 miles of scenic trails that allow riders to experience the serenity and beauty of the desert landscape up close. Individual or group rides for all levels of experience are available for either hourly or day rides. Day rides can include a tasty picnic or a cowboy cookout. Trail rides will take you into the pristine habitat of the local mountains and Indian Canyons, located on sacred ancestral tribal lands, where you will encounter historic palm oases and year-round cool streams. Please note that Smoke Tree Stables is closed in July and August.

2500 S. Toledo Ave., Palm Springs
760-327-1372
smoketreestables.com

JOIN A HIKING CLUB TREK

Greater Palm Springs is renowned for its diverse hiking opportunities, with 140 trails that traverse more than 1,250 miles. The climate during the season (October through May) is ideal for getting outdoors and enjoying our magnificent landscape and awe-inspiring beauty. A good source for information is the Desert Trails Hiking Club. You can join club members on their hikes for an annual fee of $10 for one or $15 for two or a family, which gives you membership in the club. The Coachella Valley Hiking Club also organizes several hikes per week that vary from easy to moderate to strenuous. Check the hike schedule and register for hikes on their websites. You can also get information about hiking trails from the Palm Springs Bureau of Tourism.

Coachella Valley Hiking Club	**Desert Trails Hiking Club**	**Palm Springs Bureau of Tourism**
cvhikingclub.net	deserttrailshiking.com	visitpalmsprings.com

INSIDER'S TIP

Be aware that the desert climate and landscape can be harsh and require mindfulness and preparation. Follow these simple guidelines and you'll have a richly rewarding experience: Stay on designated trails so you won't get lost. Be sure to have plenty of water, snacks, sunscreen, proper footwear, and a charged cellphone for emergencies. In summer months, hike in the morning and avoid the hottest part of the day.

Moorten Botanical Garden
Courtesy of Palm Springs Bureau of Tourism

CULTURE AND HISTORY

VISIT AN ARCHITECURAL GEM: PALM SPRINGS VISITORS CENTER

Don't miss the chance to drop in to the Palm Springs Visitors Center, which is at the city's western city limits. The Visitors Center is housed in the famed Tramway Gas Station built in 1965 by modernist architects Robson Chambers and Albert Frey.

This historic structure is on the National Register of Historic Places for its distinctive architecture and soaring roofline. As Palm Springs is world-renowned for its mid-century modern architecture, the Visitors Center is an appropriate gateway to the city. You can pick up a variety of visitor information—maps; brochures; hotel, restaurant, and recreation guides; as well as books and gifts.

2901 N. Palm Canyon Dr., Palm Springs
760-778-8418
visitpalmsprings.com

MEET A PIONEER
AT CABOT'S PUEBLO MUSEUM

One of the most unusual museums you're likely to see anywhere is Cabot's Pueblo Museum, a rambling pueblo-style dwelling of thirty-five rooms that was the homestead residence of a stalwart pioneer named Cabot Yerxa. Located in the hills of Desert Hot Springs, Cabot's Pueblo Museum is a fascinating architectural marvel that Yerxa built largely by hand from repurposed and recycled materials during a period of more than twenty years. Before he homesteaded 160 desolate acres in 1913, Yerxa was a citizen of the world, traveling to Cuba, Mexico, and Alaska and studying art in France. He was also a devoted advocate for Native Americans. Take a docent-led tour to learn about this intriguing visionary and see the collection of rare objects he amassed during his world travels.

67616 E. Desert View Ave., Desert Hot Springs
760-329-7610
cabotsmuseum.org

IMMERSE YOURSELF
IN ART AT PALM SPRINGS ART MUSEUM

One of the oldest cultural institutions in the desert is the Palm Springs Art Museum, which was founded in 1938, the same year as the city of Palm Springs itself. Visitors are frequently surprised to find a world-class museum in our small resort town. The 125,000-square-foot museum has a noteworthy art collection and presents exceptional and engaging exhibitions throughout the year. PSAM houses two outdoor sculpture gardens, a café, and the renowned Annenberg Theater, which presents a variety of performing arts. Under its cultural umbrella, PSAM has two other entities—the Architecture and Design Center, Edwards Harris Pavilion, in downtown Palm Springs; and the Palm Springs Art Museum in Palm Desert, with its four-acre Faye Sarkowsky Sculpture Garden.

Palm Springs Art Museum
101 Museum Dr., Palm Springs
760-322-4800

Palm Springs Architecture and Design Center
300 S. Palm Canyon Dr., Palm Springs
760-423-5260

Palm Springs Art Museum in Palm Desert
72-567 Hwy. 111, Palm Desert
760-346-5600

psmuseum.org

INSIDER'S TIP

The Palm Springs Art Museum hosts Free Thursdays from 4 p.m. to 8 p.m., while the other two museums—the Architecture and Design Center in Palm Springs and the Palm Springs Art Museum in Palm Desert—are free daily. The free admission policy may continue depending upon special underwriting; check the website or call. PSAMPD's Faye Sarkowsky Sculpture Garden is free and open year-round; download a guide for a self-guided garden tour.

JOIN
THE BACKSTREET ART DISTRICT
ART WALK

Discover a small but dynamic enclave of artist-owned galleries and working studios at the Backstreet Art District, located off the beaten path on a side street from East Palm Canyon Drive. You'll find a vibrant art scene and original works in a variety of media, including paintings, ceramics, jewelry, sculpture, and photography, all in one location. Stop in during the Backstreet Art District's Art Walk on the first Wednesday of each month during the "season." The Art Walk is a convivial evening that takes place from 6 p.m. to 9 p.m. and gives you an opportunity to meet and chat with the artists, visit working studios, and enjoy refreshments while perusing (and possibly buying) high-quality works of art.

2600 S. Cherokee Way, Palm Springs
backstreetartdistrict.com

TAKE A HISTORIC
WALKING TOUR

Take one of Palm Springs Historical Society's nine seasonal Historic Walking Tours to hear entertaining tales of intrigue about Palm Springs's glamorous history, culture, architecture, and local tribal legacy. You'll also learn interesting stories about many of the celebrities who have made their home here. The tours take you on a casual stroll through notable and historic neighborhoods with a knowledgeable docent, who will regale you with fascinating tidbits about local lore and celebrities who have lived, loved, and played in the Palm Springs oasis. The tours are offered during the "season" (October through April).

P.S. Walk With Me also offers walking tours curated by lifelong local resident Jade Nelson for groups of two to twelve.

Historic Walking Tours
Palm Springs Historical Society, 221 S. Palm Canyon Dr., Palm Springs
760-323-8297
pshistoricalsociety.org

P.S. Walk With Me
760-567-4696
pswalk.com

SEE PUBLIC ART
IN PALM DESERT

In Palm Desert, you'll find more than 150 works of public art throughout the city, all part of the city's Art in Public Places program. You'll see paintings, water features, and sculptures by renowned and local professional artists. You can enjoy a self-guided tour at your convenience or join a free docent-led public art tour one Saturday a month from September through May. Private tours for groups of more than three people can also be scheduled. Along El Paseo, Palm Desert's lively shopping corridor, you will find several blocks of large-scale public art sculptures. Drop in to the visitors' center to get started or view and print a map of all the public art from the city's website—a handy way to help you navigate around the city to enjoy this stunning collection.

73-510 Fred Waring Dr., Palm Desert
800-873-2428 or 760-568-1441
palm-desert.org/arts-entertainment/public-art

LEARN THE LANGUAGE OF FILM
AT PALM SPRINGS FILM FEST

For a region the size of Greater Palm Springs, the number of film festivals hosted here rivals that of most major cities. The highest profile is the Palm Springs International Film Festival, held each January. It began in 1990 and has since garnered the respect of the film industry, becoming known as a reliable source for handicapping Oscar winners. The ten-day PSIFF presents upward of two hundred international films; in addition, it's one of the only places you can view all the Academy Award nominees for Best Foreign Language Film. The PSIFF black-tie gala draws an impressive roster of A-list actors whose films are in contention for Oscar consideration. The PSIFF is presented under the auspices of the Palm Springs International Film Society, which hosts screenings and events throughout the year.

Festival office: 1700 E. Tahquitz Canyon Way, Suite 3, Palm Springs
760-322-2930 or 800-898-7256
psfilmfest.org

SEE MORE
CELEBRATIONS OF CINEMA

If you miss the Palm Springs International Film Festival in January, not to worry—there are several other specialty film festivals throughout the year. The Palm Springs International Film Society presents the annual Palm Springs International ShortFest (June), the largest festival of its kind in the United States. The ShortFest focuses on a variety of media and genres, including action, comedies, documentaries, dramas, horror stories, thrillers, and mysteries. Cinema Diverse: The Palm Springs LGBTQ Film Festival (September) takes place at the Palm Springs Cultural Center and presents the best in LGBTQ cinema. The Native FilmFest (March) is produced by the Agua Caliente Cultural Museum and showcases the best in films by, about, and starring Native Americans and other indigenous peoples from around the world.

Palm Springs International ShortFest
Festival office: 1700 E. Tahquitz Canyon Way, Suite 3, Palm Springs
760-322-2930 or 800-898-7256
psfilmfest.org

Cinema Diverse
760-880-4921
cinemadiverse.org

Native FilmFest
760-778-1079
accmuseum.org

REVEL IN THE ARTS
AT LA QUINTA ARTS FEST

The climate and clarity of light have long been reasons so many artists have found artistic inspiration in the stark beauty of the desert landscape. These factors have resulted in a dynamic and exciting art environment in Greater Palm Springs, which hosts numerous art events and festivals. The La Quinta Arts Foundation, founded in 1982, presents the La Quinta Arts Festival (March), which features three days of art exhibits, live entertainment, and wonderful food. You can see the work of more than two hundred artists from around the United States and abroad. Check the website for dates.

760-564-1244
lqaf.com

PERUSE THE WORLD
OF ART

Around the desert communities you'll find several other impressive and fun art events throughout the season. Most augment the visitor experience with live music in sunny outdoor settings. The Rancho Mirage Art Affaire is a weekend celebration of art, food, and entertainment in November. The Southwest Arts Festival in January presents a three-day event with nearly three hundred artists. Art Palm Springs, held in February, features galleries from around the country and abroad exhibiting modern and contemporary art in a variety of media. The Indian Wells Arts Festival, a three-day juried festival held in April, presents the work of two hundred artists from around the world.

Rancho Mirage Art Affaire
Rancho Mirage Community Park
71-560 San Jacinto Dr., Rancho Mirage
760-324-4511
ranchomirageca.gov/art-affaire

Southwest Arts Festival
Empire Polo Club
81800 Ave. 51, Indio
760-347-0676
discoverindio.com/southwest-arts-festival

Art Palm Springs
Palm Springs Convention Center
277 N. Avenida Caballeros, Palm Springs
800-563-7632
art-palmsprings.com

Indian Wells Arts Festival
Indian Wells Tennis Garden
78-200 Miles Ave., Indian Wells
760-346-0042
indianwellsartsfestival.com

TAKE AN
ARCHITECTURE TOUR

Learn about Palm Springs's historic mid-century modern architectural heritage through a privately guided tour. They offer an excellent overview of the city's notable commercial and residential mid-century modern architecture. The tours are conducted for groups of six in comfortable vehicles and range from ninety minutes to three hours. Each tour operator is exceptionally knowledgeable about the city's architecture and offers slightly different tours with an individual focus. Some tours are strictly exterior tours, while some offer interior tours of a couple of homes or buildings. But each will provide an illuminating and even entertaining overview of many of Palm Springs's architectural gems, and you'll learn some fascinating historical tidbits about many film, music, and literary luminaries.

The Modern Tour
760-904-0904
themoderntour.com

Palm Springs Mod Squad
Architecture & Design Tours
760-469-9265
psmodsquad.com

INSIDER'S TIP
You can also download an app for a self-driving tour of Palm Springs's modern architecture. The app is narrated by local architecture historians and has more than eighty architectural landmarks. Download the app at itunes.apple.com/us/app/palm-springs-modernism-tour/id576934996?mt=8

LEARN PRESIDENTIAL
HISTORY AT SUNNYLANDS

The Annenberg Retreat at Sunnylands is a spectacular two-hundred-acre site in Rancho Mirage that was the former private residence of the late power couple Walter and Leonore Annenberg. The Annenbergs were legendary for hosting presidents, royalty, and numerous heads of state. Today, Sunnylands carries on the Annenbergs' mission "to address serious issues facing the nation and the world community" by hosting diplomatic summits for current and future presidents. As president, Barack Obama convened several international diplomatic summits at Sunnylands. The Center and Gardens are free and open to the public Thursday through Sunday (September through June) and feature a theater, a gift store, and a café, as well as expansive postcard gardens. The center also hosts free exhibits, concerts, films, and Friday yoga classes. The 25,000-square-foot Annenberg residence, a mid-century modern marvel built in 1966, is open for tours by reservation.

37977 Bob Hope Dr., Rancho Mirage
760-202-2222
sunnylands.org

LEARN COACHELLA VALLEY HISTORY
AT HISTORY MUSEUM

Since 1965, a dedicated group of volunteers of the Coachella Valley Historical Society has kept a large archive of local history, including photographs, artifacts, and memorabilia. They opened the Coachella Valley History Museum in 1984. Open from October 1 to May 31, the Coachella Valley History Museum is a slice of living history about the agricultural heritage and the development of the Coachella Valley. Each spring, the museum hosts a free Heritage Festival in Old Town Indio, with an antique car show, exhibits, food, and a variety of live entertainment. Visit the website for a calendar of special events and exhibits.

82616 Miles Ave., Indio
760-342-6651
cvhm.org

FUN FACT
It's believed that the name of the region, "Coachella" Valley, was the result of a simple spelling error by early mapmakers for the Southern Pacific Railroad in the late 1880s. The original reference to the area was "Conchilla," meaning "seashell" in Spanish, named so because of the fossilized mollusk shells that lived in an ancient body of water; shells can still be found in the area. Despite the spelling error, the name Coachella stuck.

TAKE A CULTURAL JOURNEY
AT LA QUINTA MUSEUM

The City of La Quinta is one of the only cities in the area that has grown up around a historic resort instead of the other way around. When the famed La Quinta Resort opened in 1926, it was located in a remote patch of desert with little population. This history is chronicled at the La Quinta Museum, which is both a central repository for La Quinta's archival and historical collection and a cultural center for the city's visitors and residents. The museum, which is open year-round and is operated by the City of La Quinta, hosts a variety of cultural events throughout the year. Grab a brown bag lunch and enjoy a recorded TED Talk. Or attend a First Friday Concert, one of the museum's live music concerts. The museum also hosts book discussions with the Gallery Book Club, children's story time, and craft classes.

77-885 Avenida Montezuma, La Quinta
760-564-1283
laquintahistoricalsociety.com/la-quinta-museum

TOUR COLORFUL
WALL MURALS

In every Coachella Valley city you'll find public art murals, but in Coachella and Indio you'll find a treasure trove. There are dozens of stunning murals in these eastern Coachella Valley communities celebrating the towns' history and cultural heritage.

Long before the notoriety of the Coachella Music and Arts Festival, the region had a proud heritage as a vital agricultural community. This is where farmworkers' rights activist Cesar Chavez began his lifelong cause. These striking large-scale murals pay homage to many cultural themes and beautifully capture the history, the spirit, and the culture of their respective cities.

Palm Springs also has several distinctive wall murals that dot the city's landscape. You can download a map to these murals from the cities' websites. Or create your own self-guided walking tour of these vibrant murals. Check the photo gallery and locations at the following link.

palmspringslife.com/murals-tour-palm-springs

REMEMBER OUR VETERANS
AT PALM SPRINGS AIR MUSEUM

For US military and aviation history buffs, a visit to the Palm Springs Air Museum is a must. The Air Museum is a living history museum housed in three climate-controlled airplane hangars, with more than forty vintage World War II warbirds and rare Korean War and Vietnam-era airplanes; many are still operational. The museum has a theater and a café and also contains exhibits, photographs, and video footage that tell the history of America's military involvement during the Korean War, World War II, and the Vietnam War. Many of the volunteer docents are veterans of these wars. You can also experience the thrill of riding in one of its vintage C-47 Skytrain and P-51 Mustang warbirds. The Palm Springs Air Museum has been named one of the world's top aviation museums by CNN.

745 N. Gene Autry Trail, Palm Springs
760-778-6262
palmspringsairmuseum.org

CELEBRATE
MODERNISM WEEK

The City of Palm Springs is world-renowned for its astonishing preponderance of mid-century modern architecture—structures that were built from the 1930s through the 1960s. In fact, Palm Springs boasts more mid-century modern architecture than any other place in the world. To this end, the city celebrates its architectural heritage with Modernism Week. The eleven-day festival features modernist design, architecture, fashion, and more. There are multiple home and garden tours, lectures, parties, films, and the Modernism Show and Sale, which features more than eighty exhibitors. Held twice a year in October and February, Modernism Week annually draws more than 100,000 people from around the world. Many other cities in the Coachella Valley also participate. Check the website for dates, a list of events, and tickets.

modernismweek.com

TOUR THE HISTORIC
O'DONNELL HOUSE

Palm Springs has not only a celebrated architectural heritage but also a rich and fascinating cultural history told through a tour of the historic O'Donnell House, which is listed on the National Register of Historic Places. Enjoy a ninety-minute docent-led tour of this extraordinary, meticulously restored home, built in 1925. The tour of the O'Donnell House, also known as Ojo del Desierto, or "Eye of the Desert," recounts the history of Palm Springs as seen from high on the hillside above the Palm Springs Art Museum. The house also features a fine collection of Mission-style furnishings, including rare tiles, pottery, and early California furniture. The O'Donnell House was spotlighted in actress Diane Keaton's 2007 book *California Romantica*, which chronicled rare California Mission and Spanish Colonial homes.

800-966-9597
odonnellhouse.com

VISIT HISTORIC ADOBE
AT A HISTORICAL SOCIETY

Visit an authentic adobe structure that houses the Palm Springs Historical Society, which is located at downtown's Village Green, a collection of historic buildings and museums open for public tours. Since 1955, the PSHS has been the archival and curatorial keeper of Palm Springs's fascinating and colorful history. The Palm Springs Historical Society operates two of Palm Springs's oldest buildings—the McCallum Adobe, which was built in 1884 and houses the society's exhibits, and the Cornelia White House, built in 1893—both open for tours. Both museums are free to the public and are open from October to May. The Historical Society of Palm Desert is also an impressive repository for the city's archives, historical photos, and an oral history of Palm Desert pioneers.

Palm Springs Historical Society
221 S. Palm Canyon Dr., Palm Springs
760-323-8297
pshistoricalsociety.org

Historical Society of Palm Desert
72-861 El Paseo Dr., Palm Desert
760-346-6588
hspd.org

LISTEN UP
AT A SPEAKER SERIES

If you think Greater Palm Springs is just a pretty face, think again. Besides fun in the sun we enjoy intellectual stimulation, too. We have several notable speaker series that are held during the "season," generally from October/November to April/May.

One of the longest-running is the Desert Town Hall Speaker Series, which draws high-profile international and nationally known authors, world leaders, and cultural trendsetters. VIP tickets include a meet and greet with the speaker. Tickets must be purchased in advance, as they sell out quickly.

The Rancho Mirage Speaker Series and Palm Springs Speaks, presented by the City of Rancho Mirage and the Palm Springs Library, respectively, also offer engaging programs with exceptional authors, entertainers, and political figures. Each speaker series provides audiences the opportunity to participate in Q&As with these nationally known personalities.

Desert Town Hall
Renaissance Indian Wells Resort
44-400 Indian Wells Lane, Indian Wells
760-610-2852
deserttownhall.org

**Palm Springs Library:
Palm Springs Speaks**
held in two venues, check website
760-624-8752
palmspringsspeaks.org

Rancho Mirage Speaker Series
Eisenhower Medical Center
39000 Bob Hope Dr., Rancho Mirage
760-324-4511
rmspeakerseries.com

STROLL THROUGH
MOORTEN BOTANICAL GARDEN

Take time to visit the enchanting historic grounds of Moorten Botanical Garden, which was a favorite Palm Springs attraction of the late Huell Howser, the PBS-TV host. The gardens were established by Chester "Cactus Slim" and Patricia Moorten in 1938, the same year the City of Palm Springs was founded. These early Palm Springs residents created a truly unique garden of three thousand cacti and succulents, some of which are available for purchase. The botanical garden, now operated by their son, Clark Moorten, is situated on more than an acre, with walkways, water features, ancient fossils, and other historic relics throughout the meandering gardens. Don't miss what perhaps might be the world's only "cactarium," which features rare specimens from deserts around the world. The family home, a historic Spanish Mediterranean structure, is now used for private events and weddings.

1701 S. Palm Canyon Dr., Palm Springs
760-327-6555
moortenbotanicalgarden.com

INSIDER'S TIP

Desert X had its enormously successful inaugural event in 2017. Desert X will be produced on a biannual basis and will showcase the work of international artists who create site-specific works inspired by the desert landscape. Check website for dates and events.

desertx.org

Courtesy of Roger Morales for Palm Springs Life

SHOPPING AND FASHION

BE JUST FABULOUS

Along a tony stretch of North Palm Canyon in Palm Springs is the Uptown Design District, a fun shopping and dining corridor. As the name implies, the Uptown Design District captures the zeitgeist of trend-setting fashions, stylish home decor, and collectible mid-century modern furnishings, as well as popular high-style eateries. The first of many Trina Turk Boutiques opened in Palm Springs in 2002. The district runs along North Palm Canyon from Alejo Road north to Vista Chino Drive, a distance of a little more than a mile, which makes a visit to the Uptown Design District a comfortable and walkable experience. Stop for lunch at any of the acclaimed restaurants, grab an excellent coffee, or treat yourself to a refreshing craft cocktail along the way. Just Fabulous is a fun, adventurous place to shop and browse books, cards, gifts, apparel, and more. Be Just Fabulous is the store motto.

Trina Turk Boutique
891 N. Palm Canyon Dr., Palm Springs
760-416-2856
trinaturk.com

Just Fabulous
515 N. Palm Canyon Dr., Palm Springs
760-864-1300
bjustfabulous.com

WATCH THE RUNWAY
AT FASHION WEEK

The annual Fashion Week El Paseo, held each March, is a highly anticipated signature event of the "season" in the Coachella Valley. Fashion Week El Paseo is the largest annual fashion event on the West Coast and features a week-long series of runway shows, receptions, after-parties, trunk shows, and meet-and-greet opportunities with former and present *Project Runway* designers. Since its inception more than ten years ago, Fashion Week El Paseo, so named for its location in the El Paseo shopping district in Palm Desert, has showcased the work of both renowned and emerging couture designers in nightly runway shows. Unlike other fashion weeks around the country and throughout the world, Fashion Week El Paseo is geared to the public. Check the website for dates and to purchase tickets.

760-325-2333
fashionweekelpaseo.com

SHOP EL PASEO

The El Paseo Shopping District in Palm Desert will please the most discriminating shopaholics with its mile-long boulevard and three hundred shops. You'll be able to choose from a dizzying variety of boutiques and retailers specializing in jewelry, apparel, art, and home decor and more than two dozen restaurants and cafés. Nearly every luxury brand has a presence on El Paseo, including Tiffany & Co., Louis Vuitton, Burberry, Escada, St. John, Gucci, and Ralph Lauren. But modest budgets will also find reason to shop 'til you drop, with retailers such as Chico's, Talbots, Banana Republic, and Tommy Bahama. The Gardens on El Paseo provide a relaxing respite in their beautifully landscaped gardens and courtyards, which often feature live concerts. Check the website for a schedule of special events.

palm-desert.org/things-to-do/el-paseo

FIND A TREASURE
AT COD STREET FAIR

For more than thirty years, the Street Fair at College of the Desert has been a favorite weekend tradition for residents and visitors alike. The Street Fair is a colorful and festive outdoor shopping bazaar held on the College of the Desert campus. You'll find more than three hundred merchant and artist booths, live entertainment, gourmet food, and a farmers market in winter months. You'll have fun perusing a huge selection of offerings at great prices, including clothing, art, furniture, pottery, jewelry, leather goods, home decor, pet accessories, crafts, and gourmet specialty items, plus plants and flowers. The Street Fair is open on Saturdays and Sundays year-round. From October to May hours are 7 a.m. to 2 p.m., and from June to September hours are 7 a.m. to noon.

43-500 Monterey Ave., Palm Desert
codaastreetfair.com

COLLECT RETRO FINDS
AT PALM SPRINGS VINTAGE MARKET

If you're a fan of retro, vintage, or mid-century modern style, the Palm Springs Vintage Market is for you. Held the first Sunday of the month from 8 a.m. to 2 p.m. (October through May) in the shaded parking area of the Palm Springs Cultural Center, the Vintage Market is a fun treasure-hunting experience. Vendor booths display a variety of wares, such as vintage clothing, jewelry, home furnishings, toys and collectibles, furniture, records, and assorted retro memorabilia. Spend a leisurely morning perusing retro objets d'art while enjoying live music and meeting friendly folks who share your interest in the unusual and rare.

Palm Springs Cultural Center, 2300 E. Baristo Rd., Palm Springs
760-534-7968
palmspringsvintagemarket.com

JOIN THE FUN
AT VILLAGEFEST

The historic town of Palm Springs is proud of its small-village feel. Every Thursday evening, you can celebrate VillageFest when the main downtown thoroughfare, Palm Canyon Drive, is closed to vehicular traffic for several blocks (from Baristo Road to Amado Road). VillageFest celebrated its twenty-fifth anniversary in 2016 and has been a weekly year-round tradition for locals and visitors, who flock downtown for the festival atmosphere. You can shop for hand-crafted art, gift items, and fresh produce. There are also lots of food concessions and live music, creating a lively family- and dog-friendly event. VillageFest takes place from 6 p.m. to 10 p.m. from October through May and from 7 p.m. to 10 p.m. June through September.

villagefest.org

SNAG A BARGAIN
AT DESERT HILLS PREMIUM OUTLETS

Just twenty minutes east of Palm Springs you'll find the Desert Hills Premium Outlets, ground zero for fashionistas and home to the largest collection of luxury outlets in California. Desert Hills is located in Cabazon, where you can shop at nearly two hundred designer outlets, such as Alexander McQueen, Dolce & Gabbana, Gucci, Helmut Lang, Jimmy Choo, Neiman Marcus Last Call, Polo Ralph Lauren Factory Store, Prada, Saint Laurent Paris, Saks Fifth Avenue OFF 5TH, Salvatore Ferragamo, Versace, and many more. Take a break from your bargain shopping at the food courts or nearby restaurants and the famous Hadley Fruit Orchards, a roadside institution since 1951. Desert Hills Premium Outlets are open Monday through Saturday from 10 a.m. to 9 p.m. and Sunday from 10 a.m. to 8 p.m.

48400 Seminole Dr., Cabazon
951-849-5018 or 951-849-6641
premiumoutlets.com/outlet/desert-hills

INSIDER'S TIP

Stop by the Desert Hills Premium Outlets administration office and pick up a VIP shopping pass that will give you extra savings in designated stores. And check the website to learn about special promotions individual stores may be offering.

GO RESALE SHOPPING
AT REVIVALS

For bargain hunters, consignment shopping is about the most fun you can have. And the Coachella Valley is famous for its numerous superb consignment retailers, which you'll find in every city. Whether it's clothing, furniture, or housewares you're looking for, you'll be bound to discover a treasure trove of great finds. And if you're on the hunt for vintage and/or resale designer fashions, you're in luck. During the past few years, the Coachella Valley has become renowned among savvy fashionistas and TV and film producers as the place to score killer resale vintage clothing and designer fashions. Here are just some to check out—happy hunting!

The Frippery
664 N. Palm Canyon Dr., Palm Springs
760-699-5365
thefrippery.com

Revivals Resale Mart
611 S. Palm Canyon Dr., Palm Springs
760-318-6491
Several other locations are listed on the website.
revivalsstores.com

Marga's Repeat Boutique
73900 El Paseo, #3 Rear, Palm Desert
760-773-1988
margasrepeatboutique.com

EXPERIENCE ARTFUL SHOPPING
AT A MUSEUM STORE

One of the best-kept secrets about museums is their gift shops. They often have unusual and fabulous finds. The Palm Springs Art Museum store is no exception. The Museum Store has a selection of one-of-a-kind custom jewelry, creative and educational toys, stylish home decor, art books, and fun gift ideas you won't see elsewhere. The store also hosts occasional trunk shows that showcase the work of national and international studio artists and give the public the rare opportunity to purchase their hand-crafted, one-of-a-kind designs. Likewise, the PSAM's other shop, the Architecture and Design Center's Bradford W. Bates Vault: The Museum Design Store (so named because it's housed in a former bank vault), sells architecture and design books and unique jewelry and gift items that showcase exceptional contemporary design.

Museum Store
Palm Springs Art Museum, 101 Museum Dr., Palm Springs
760-322-4800
psmuseum.org/museum-store

The Bradford W. Bates Vault: The Museum Design Store
Architecture and Design Center, 300 S. Palm Canyon Dr., Palm Springs
760-423-5264
psmuseum.org/architecture-design-center/store

FIND NEW
SHOPPING ADVENTURES

What would a vacay or getaway be without some retail therapy? Whether you're a resident or a visitor to our magnificent desert, shopping options abound. There's nothing like a shopping break from outdoor recreation, cultural enhancement, or poolside R&R to renew the spirit!

As Greater Palm Springs grows as a tourism destination, more and more amenities pop up, and shopping options are a big part of the mix.

Around the valley, there are numerous new retailers, and in the new Palm Springs downtown project you'll find a bevy of new stores. Listed here are only a few to inspire you.

Chelsea Lane Swimwear
170 N. Palm Canyon Dr.
Palm Springs
760-278-1278
chelsealane.com

Blonde Clothing Boutique
111 N. Palm Canyon Dr., Suite 130
Palm Springs
760-318-3400
blondeclothingboutique.com

Peepa's: Lifestyle Experience
108 S. Indian Canyon Dr.
Palm Springs
760-318-3553
peepasps.com

Candice Held Boutiques
73080 El Paseo, Ste. 2, Palm Desert
1345 N. Palm Canyon Dr.
Palm Springs
760-340-0430
candiceheld.com

BE INSPIRED
AT PEREZ ART AND DESIGN CENTER

It may come as a surprise when you arrive at the Perez Art and Design Center that you are in a dynamic enclave of some of the best vintage shopping in Southern California. Located in an unassuming strip mall in a Cathedral City industrial neighborhood, this spot has been discovered by LA and New York designers and has even caught the attention of *Vogue* magazine. Located on Perez Road, the design hub comprises several notable shops specializing in mid-century modern decor—the undisputable brand of Palm Springs. Among these über-cool shops are Hedge, which has a following of discriminating collectors from all over Southern California; JP Denmark, which, as the name implies, offers vintage Danish modern; and At Hōm, which has a variety of new and vintage furnishings and accessories.

Hedge	**JP Denmark**
68-929 Perez Rd., Unit F	68-929 Perez Rd., Unit N
Cathedral City	Cathedral City
760-770-0090	760-408-9147
hedgepalmsprings.com	jpantik.com

At Hōm
68-929 Perez Rd., Unit GHI, Cathedral City
760-770-4447
at-hom.com

● ●

WADE
THROUGH THE RIVER

The River in Rancho Mirage brings together the synergy of an exciting shopping, dining, and entertainment destination. The center's unusual design is a big part of the fun, with a large body of water that snakes around the buildings, creating an inviting oasis. Shopping options abound here, and you can also catch a film at a multi-screen movie theater, listen to a musical performance in the River's amphitheater, treat yourself to an ice-cream cone, relax with a cappuccino on the plaza, or dine at one of several eateries.

71-800 Hwy. 111, Rancho Mirage
760-341-2711
theriveratranchomirage.com

Palm Springs Visitors Center
Courtesy of Palm Springs Bureau of Tourism

SUGGESTED
ITINERARIES

EXPLORE OUTDOORS

Walk in Ancient Footsteps at Indian Canyons, 58

Catch a Fish at Whitewater Preserve, 60

Hike the Thousand Palms Oasis, 59

Venture into the San Andreas Fault, 62

Get Back in the Saddle at Smoke Tree Stables, 90

Join a Hiking Club Trek, 91

Visit New National Monuments, 67

Learn Presidential History at Sunnylands, 107

Immerse Yourself in Art at Palm Springs Art Museum, 96

Stroll through Moorten Botanical Garden, 116

FAMILY-FRIENDLY FUN

Ride the Waves at Wet 'n Wild, 87

Take a Balloon Ride at Hot Air Balloon Festival, 80

Take a Thrill Ride at Aerial Tramway, 55

Join the Fun at VillageFest, 125

Take a Walk on the Living Desert's Wild Side, 63

TASTY TREATS

CATCH THE VIEWS

HIGH DESERT ADVENTURE

RETRO AND VINTAGE SHOPPING

DIVINE DESIGN

LOVE TO SHOP

O'Donnell Golf Course
Courtesy of Palm Springs Bureau of Tourism

INDEX